Praise for John Lees' work and
, field

~~A~~ ~~ees~~ has a rare talent: he combines absolute mastery of his specialist ~~with~~ a clear, reader-friendly writing style. John's books are a joy ~~d~~ as well as an indispensable roadmap for anyone serious about ~~aging~~ their careers.

Steve Crabb, Editor, People Management

~~ghly~~ recommended – always practical, but never patronising.

Ian Wylie, Editor, Guardian Rise

Work has come to mean a lot more than a career ladder and a salary, and nobody understands that better than John Lees. He can help you find your direction – and give you the strategies to reach your destination.

Maureen Rice, Editor, PSYCHOLOGIES

John Lees inspires people to rethink the way they work: to work with greater purpose, meaning and life/work balance.

Andrea Watson, Editor, Daily Express CAREERS

Career advice with a difference, John Lees delivers a clear and comprehensive step-by-step guide to making your dream job a reality.

Sam Dukes, Editor, EDGE
(Institute of Leadership & Management)

You can always rely on John Lees to come up with helpful, practical advice that is both accessible and effective.

Terry Gibson, Editor, AMED Organisations & People

I love John's straight-up approach. There's nothing airy-fairy about the career advice in his books and yet the tone holds your interest, not the usual dry-as-a-bone business book banter. What I love most is that it's real-life, real-world stuff: first he guides you to making your own career decisions with passion and instinct but then he gives professional, realistic – and very grown up – advice about making those decisions happen. I can still remember reading *How to Get a Job You'll Love* as a young journalist fresh off the boat from Oz with zilch industry contacts. Now I am in my dream job – John's advice works, pure and simple.

Anna Magee, Health Editor, RED

Take Control of Your Career is recommended reading for anyone serious about their professional development.
Philip McMullan, Editor, The Recruitment Consultant

A brilliant book for anyone who wants a new direction.
Tessa Hilton, Editor at Large, Woman & Home

John Lees continues to write books that are practical, engaging and inspiring.
Sandra, Workplace Journalist

A great way to kick-start your career makeover.
Cosmopolitan

What sets John Lees apart from other careers authors writing at the moment is his ability to present solutions to, what can be, pretty complex problems, in a straightforward, user-friendly manner.
Michael Brash, Editor, Care Appointments Scotland

As an expert in the field, John combines his comprehensive knowledge of the world of work with a dynamic positive attitude. He is my first port of call for careers advisory topics.
Catherine Quinn, Guardian and The Times Employment Journalist

In the new and, at times, confusing work landscape of the 21st Century, John Lees continues to be a solid and reliable source of vital information and guidance for anyone who is serious about making the right career decisions.
Sally Longson, Careers Coach and Writer

John Lees unfailingly offers clear, accessible career guidelines.
Penny Cottee, Business and Careers Journalist

John Lees advice is witty, incisive and really works – a real breath of fresh air for those who want to change the course of their working lives.
Tessa Williams, Journalist and Contributor of EVE Magazine

Take Control of Your Career offers a fresh and original look at how and why you can influence the direction your career takes: thought provoking and free of jargon.
Emma Lunn, Journalist

John Lees uses his considerable experience of the world of work to write practical and readable books that can help you move forward in your career. He's also very useful if you want great quotes for careers features.

Adeline Iziren, Regular Guardian Contributor and Founder of Smartgrads.co.uk

John Lees produces books which are inspirational. They are easy to read and make sense to everyday life. His writing is challenging and thought-provoking whilst never moving out of the real world. Any John Lees book is a must if you are planning your career.

Amanda Green, Careers Coach and Reviewer for Career Guidance Today Magazine

John's books are cleverly written. He knows there's only one person who can make all the right career and life choices for yourself and that's you. His job is to make sure you put in all the hard work necessary to come up with the right solutions while thinking you're having a fun and enjoyable read.

Charlotte Hindle, Freelance Travel Writer (career breaks and gap years)

John Lees is a regular presenter at the forum3 volunteering and recruitment event where he has delivered successful seminars based on his books which are always popular and well attended sessions.

Debbie Hockham, Event Director, forum3.co.uk

Becoming responsible for your own career is fine but nobody tells you how ... until now. John Lees shows how to progress within the organisation and turn a job into a success story. I recommend it most highly.

Robin H D Wood, Managing Director, Career Management Consultants Limited

Take Control of Your Career

Take Control
of Your Career

John Lees

The McGraw·Hill Companies

London • Burr Ridge IL • New York • St Louis • San Francisco • Auckland
Bogotá • Caracas • Lisbon • Madrid • Mexico • Milan
Montreal • New Delhi • Panama • Paris • San Juan • São Paulo
Singapore • Sydney • Tokyo • Toronto

The *McGraw·Hill* Companies

Take Control of Your Career
John Lees

An adaptation of John Lees' *How to Get the Perfect Promotion*

ISBN 0077109678

 **Professional**

Published by McGraw-Hill Professional
Shoppenhangers Road
Maidenhead
Berkshire
SL6 2QL
Telephone: 44 (0) 1628 502 500
Fax: 44 (0) 1628 770 224
Website: www.mcgraw-hill.co.uk

British Library Cataloguing in Publication Data
A catalogue record for this book is available from the British Library

Library of Congress Cataloguing in Publication Data
The Library of Congress data for this book has been applied for from the Library of Congress

Text design by Robert Gray
Produced by Gray Publishing, Tunbridge Wells, Kent
Printed and bound in UK by CPI Bath Press

About the Author

John Lees is one of the UK's best-known career coaches. *How To Get A Job You'll Love* was WH Smith's business book of the month in January 2003, and regularly tops the list as the best-selling careers book by a British author.

As a career transition coach, he specializes in helping people make difficult career decisions: either difficult because they don't know what to do next, or because there are barriers in the way to success. Careers workshops have been delivered in the USA, South Africa and Ireland, and John regularly speaks at UK events (Times Crème, Total Jobs Live, and Next Steps) and has also featured as a speaker at the world's largest international career conferences in the USA.

He writes regularly for *The Times, The Guardian, Personnel Today* and *Pathfinder,* and his work has been featured on TV, radio and in many publications including *Management Today, Cosmopolitan, The Daily Express Real World, Financial World, People Management, Pathfinder, Eve,* and *She.*

John is a graduate of the universities of Cambridge and London and has spent most of his career focusing on the world of work. He has trained recruitment specialists since the mid-1980s, and is the former Chief Executive of the Institute of Employment Consultants (now the Recruitment & Employment Confederation, REC). He now runs his own careers consultancy and is also retained as Senior Associate (Learning and Career Development) to outplacement specialists Career Management Consultants Ltd.

As an ordained Anglican priest John works as volunteer clergy in the Diocese of Chester, and has a particular interest in vocations and the spiritual dimension of work. He lives and works in Cheshire, with his wife, the children's writer, Jan Dean, and their two sons.

See www.jobyoulove.co.uk for further checklists and details of John's other books by McGraw-Hill. For details of workshops and one-to-one coaching from John Lees Associates see www.johnleescareers.com or telephone 01565 631625.

ACKNOWLEDGEMENTS

While all the errors and omissions in this book are my own, my gratitude goes to all those whose feedback or ideas helped shape this book, including: Stuart Robertson and Derek Wilkie of Stuart Robertson Associates, Daniel Porot, Dick Bolles, Stuart McIntosh, Philip Spencer, Carole Pemberton, Liz Cross, and Ian Webb. Thanks to Janie Wilson and Mary Maybin of Passport and to Robin Wood, MD of Career Management Consultants Limited, for giving me the opportunity to road-test many of these ideas.

I am indebted to Stephanie Clark for her website research, and to Sue Blake for creating so many interesting PR conversations. Most of all I owe my editor Elizabeth Choules a huge thank you – not only for coaxing the book into existence with her usual diligence, but also for helping me absorb the results of the survey featured in Chapter 2 of this book.

My thanks, too, to all those who responded to the career survey: José Arnó, Carla Barrett, Janet Basford, Marc J Beaulieu, Penney Beazley, Peter Bell, Jo Bond, Sara Bosley, Andrew Bramley, June Burrough, Andrew Carr, Stuart Carter, Penny Chester, Linda Clark, Claire Coldwell, Andy Cole, Geoff Coombe, John Courtis, Samantha Csorba, Margaret Dale, Daniel Porot, Bill Douse, John Eardley, Mike Eastwood, Ron Feasey, John Francis, Harry Freedman, Beverley Gartside, Keith Harden, Andrée Harpur, Rob Head, Helen Green, Bill Hollyhead,

Rod Howgate, Deirdre Hughes, Stephen Hunter, Peter Jackson, Halik Kochanski, Nigel Lloyd, Fred Mahoney, Stuart McIntosh, Valerie Michej, Jane Moorhouse, Nicola Foster, Breda O'Toole, Derek Osborn, Bernard Pearce, Carole Pemberton, Lynda Pickess, David Podger, Maureen Rice-Knight, Julia Robertson, Helen Rodway, Melissa Rosati, Sally Skidmore, Alan Small, Philip Spencer, Rob Stickland, Anne Stojic, Andrew Tallents, Alan Thurm, Garth Toombs, Mike Wallwork, Linda Walmsley, Bill Walmsley, Joëlle Warren, Ian Webb, Pegi Wheatley, Derek Wilkie, Justine Wilkinson, Robin Wood, and Doreen Wright.

This book is dedicated to my sons Matthew and Christopher, both now stepping out into the career jungle.

Contents

Taking Control

This chapter helps you to:

■ Look at better methods of shaping your career

■ Find strategies for taking control of your future

■ Understand how and why people move up the career ladder

■ Audit how satisfied you are with your present job

■ Begin to take control of your working life

Manage your future or somebody else will.

Peter Drucker

TAKING CONTROL OF YOUR FUTURE

Why do I need to be in control?

Let's begin by recognizing the simple truth that your careers teacher never told you: most careers are unplanned. The majority of workers in skilled or professional jobs will admit their career history has been constructed by a series of fairly random events. The problem is that this often leads us into a piece of 'all or nothing' thinking: either we have a full and developed career plan, or we do without one completely.

Whatever kind of work you do, your workplace has probably altered radically in the past decade, and will change even more dramatically in the next 10 years. How, you might ask, can you hope to plan your working future when no-one seems to have a clear idea of what changes will come along next? How do you plan career steps, have a strategy for development, job growth, or promotion? If long-term planning seems futile, it's tempting to do nothing. However, the steps you take in the next 12 months, if you really start to take control of your working life, will probably have more effect on your future than anything else you have done.

This book is designed to help you to follow in the footsteps of people who have taken control to develop or move into more stimulating work. There are many approaches, but here are some of the most effective.

People who take control of their own careers

▮ Learn from other people's career stories (see **Chapter 2**).

▮ Have a clear insight into their own personal goals (see **Chapter 3**).

▮ Have learned the art of DIY career coaching (see **Chapter 3**).

▮ Understand what motivates them (see **Chapter 4**).

▮ Find an ever-increasing range of ways of showing how they add value to their organization (see **Chapter 5**).

▮ Communicate how they closely match the needs of their organization (see **Chapter 5**).

▮ Understand how they are perceived by others and learn how to manage those perceptions by focusing on key events and being visible to key influencers (see **Chapter 6**).

▮ Learn how to adapt their jobs, and keep on improving them (see **Chapter 7**).

▮ Have found the right energy balance between work, personal relationships, learning, fun, and rest (see **Chapter 8**).

▮ Have the tools to negotiate job content, advancement, and pay (see **Chapter 9**).

▌ Learn how to avoid career traps and career-limiting actions (see **Chapter 10**).

▌ Know how important it is to make an impact quickly when you start a new job (see **Chapter 11**).

▌ ... and also know when it's time to jump ship (see **Chapter 12**).

Career enhancement

There are many terms to describe ways of taking control of your career: career development is the one usually adopted by organizations. This book will emphasize several terms. The first is **Career awareness** (see **Chapter 3**) – an approach that gets away from conventional career planning. Naturally, this book will also talk about different methods of building on your career and ways of taking control. However, a key phrase that you'll keep coming across is **career enhancement**. This is about taking control so that your career moves in a direction that matches your personal agenda.

Time and energy

In the 1930s, the economist John Maynard Keynes predicted that we would be working an average of 5 hours a week by the end of the century. This sounds outlandish now, but only 25 years ago society was planning for a hugely expanded range of leisure and educational activities because so many people were taking early retirement or working shorter weeks.

Something happened in the 1990s to change all that. A quarter of workers in the UK are employed in what is officially recognized as a 'long hours' work culture. The typical family (according to the UK's Economic & Social Research Council) is working about 20 hours a week more than it did 25 years ago. A high proportion of professional workers are putting in more than 60 hours a week. It often feels as if there just aren't enough hours in the day to meet targets, attend meetings, read and answer all those e-mails. There always seems too little time to commit even a few hours to career planning.

Think about your life energy. Just work out for a moment how many hours you are likely to spend in work during the course of a working lifetime. Typically it's about 100,000. That's an awfully long time to be watching the clock. Over 75% of our weekly energy is focused on work – preparing for work, getting to work, talking about work and worrying about work .... We only get a finite amount of energy to spend in life, so choosing how we spend the most active parts of our life is pretty important.

CHANGING THE WAY YOU THINK ABOUT YOUR CAREER

Work: a rapidly changing map

A number of other changes have transformed the world of work at high speed during the past decade, but it's worth sorting myth from reality. We *believe* that people are changing jobs more often than ever before, but in fact this is true only for some sectors. It's because we keep hearing about the decline of safe, permanent jobs that we also believe more and more people are moving out of traditional working relationships. In fact, the best predictions indicate that by 2020 most of us will still be in permanent jobs (although not necessarily full-time jobs: there has been a big increase in part-time and flexible working). On the other hand, as we will see below, workers are discovering a wider range of new working patterns and arrangements.

What are the other key features in our map of work? These are the themes that have already emerged in the early 21st century. The big six factors seem to be as follows:

1. Ageing workforce

By 2020, it's estimated in the USA that there will be over a million people past their 100th birthday. By the same date, in the UK there will be a million more people who are aged over 65 than there are under 16. Society is ageing rapidly, and there will soon be far fewer bright young things about. While a generation back we reacted to this idea by setting up the University of the Third Age, now the main concern is how long people are going to have to work before they have a sufficiently well-funded pension in order to retire.

2. Information overload

In 1910 the total amount of information in the world doubled about every 11 years. Within a decade or so this will be happening in months rather than years. We were promised the paperless office, but what we got instead was overload – more emails, more documents, more websites, more TV channels and more books than we can possibly absorb in a single lifetime. Wading through all this information is stressful and tiring, and a huge amount of working time is spent filtering and editing data in order to pick out the bits of information that we're looking for.

3. Decreasing work satisfaction

A number of surveys (for example, by the ESRC in the UK) tell us the most important fact when it comes to looking at career development: in the past decade we have become much less happy at work. The greatest area of dissatisfaction is around working hours, but whether you look at relationships with managers, company culture, or simple job satisfaction, we're significantly less happy while at work than we used to be.

4. Increasing desire for life choices

This factor has strong links with 3 above. We have become attuned not just to the idea of consumer choice, but deeply ingrained choice about all things in our lives. A lot of television airtime is given over to makeovers: house, garden, lifestyle, partners, personal appearance. We have a strong sense that we have a right to make aesthetic, personal choices about everything that surrounds us. No wonder then that we perhaps have an increased sense that we want more out of our working lives.

5. Greater social isolation

A lesser known fact is that more people in the UK and USA are living alone. By 2020 about a third of the British population will live alone. This has all kinds of economic and psychological consequences. For some, maintaining income and lifestyle will be more important. For others, a lack of social commitments will make it easier to switch to different kinds of work. Most importantly, many people will simply feel more isolated outside of work at a time when it feels like employers are offering less support in most areas. Having less support outside of work will matter when individuals have to deal with difficult work situations or make career decisions.

6. New career mindset

This coin has two faces. The first is the rather unpalatable fact that employers are far less eager than they were in the past to look after the careers of their workers. There are still a number of paternalistic employers who invest in well-designed programmes aimed at long-term development and progression, but such employers are now in a minority. The other side of the coin is the realization that millions have come to since the 1990s: it's our responsibility to manage our own careers. The new career mindset isn't just about methods, it's also about values. In surveys younger workers say that they believe that their parents' generation paid too high a price for career success (in terms of health and family relationships). However, there is also a strong wish to exercise choice, and to approach the whole idea of a career very differently.

How do these factors influence our career decisions? First, we're aiming at an ever-moving target. Work is changing, and quickly. Secondly, most of us haven't really got used to the idea of taking control, and making choices.

'CAREER': A MOVEABLE FEAST

The whole idea that we have 'careers' is relatively modern. The word 'job' originally meant 'tasks allocated for the day' – and many workers moved from one activity to another according to the needs of the marketplace. Before the mid-20th century most people had very little occupational choice. They worked locally, moving from school to work without any perceived need to match person to job. However, the growth of new, sophisticated industries and cheap transport meant that it became important for employers to make sensible decisions about selection and training. The idea of career choice was born. We are encouraged to think about the kind of work that suits us best, and how to find it.

The past decade has seen a rather contradictory new picture. Following a decade of downsizing and restructuring, workers feel less satisfied and more vulnerable to change. At the same time, as our big six factors demonstrate, we expect more out of life, including our working lives. That's why, in the past 10 years, we have seen a very new set of working arrangements:

I **Flexible working**: something that can benefit both employee and organization.

I **Shifting occupations**: something frowned on 25 years ago is increasingly seen as acceptable.

I **Portfolio working** (see below): a fundamental change in traditional employer/worker relationships.

I **Work choices that improve life/work balance**: a topic hardly ever out of the media.

I **Career breaks**: an increasing number of people are interested in taking time out from their jobs and returning to work with a new perspective.

THE FRINGE MINDSET

What do we mean by the 'fringe'? Essentially these are workers who don't work in conventional employment relationships. In the 1980s, management guru Charles Handy predicted a massive growth in temporary and contract workers that wasn't entirely fulfilled. The percentage of the workforce in these kinds of jobs hasn't changed much, and most workers are still in permanent jobs. However, there has been a significant increase in people running their own businesses (UK government statistics indicate that self-employment grew by 300,000 in 2003 and by a further 100,000 in 2004). 'Fringe' workers are those who are neither employed on permanent contracts nor fully self-employed. Society keeps finding new ways of describing the following (for far more detail of portfolio working options, see my other book *How To Get A Job You'll Love*):

I **Freelancers**: the oldest form of contract workers. Journalists and artists have worked in this way for generations. This includes those who produce products and services in their own time and offer them to the marketplace. The ability to do so has increased remarkably with the growth of the Internet.

I **Self-employed specialists**: workers who offer their specialism to a range of employers. Self-employment is seen by many as a way of taking control of their work, and working in a one-person business (known in the USA is known as a 'soleprenuer') often provides a huge degree of freedom.

I **Interim managers**: professionals who move from employer to employer, typically looking after a role or project for 2–3 months. There has been major growth in this kind of working in the past 5 years.

I **Part-time and job share**: these roles may in fact be covered by permanent contracts, but some workers use such work to support other working activities.

I **Voluntary**: increasingly sophisticated arrangements exist to connect willing volunteers with needy projects and organizations.

I **Portfolio**: a metaphor for a rich mix of some or all of the above. Portfolio workers often mix conventional employment with various forms of consultancy, voluntary, freelance or other work.

It's important to emphasize that the majority of people aren't taking these options. Most people are still in conventional working arrangements. What's interesting is the number of workers who are talking about flexible and unconventional working arrangements. The UK press has been full of stories about flexible working. At the same time we're also interested in people who really do take control of their careers by trying to directly manage the balance of activities they undertake in a working week. The fringe remains a minority, but sets the tone for the whole.

As a result, it seems, we're all more tuned into career options. The press is fascinated by stories of people making huge career changes, exotic career breaks, or giving it all up to do something exciting. Once career realignment seemed to be the kind of thing that accompanied a mid-life crisis, but now it seems we can hit a career crisis at any age.

NEW FIELDS, NEW MINDSET

Just as we are starting to think differently about *how* we work, we're also taking off the blinkers about the kinds of work that are possible. Every week it seems as though a new occupation is invented. So many roles are available now that were not there to our parents' generation: website designer, aromatherapist, life coach and so on.

Information technology has a huge impact. A principle known as Moore's Law predicts that computers double in power about every 18 months, and it still keeps on happening. This means that technology keeps getting more faster and cheaper all the time. This has huge impact on jobs. However, it's also important to realize that not all job growth has come from the high-tech sector. The fastest growing occupation in the 1990s, for example, was not (as you might predict) telephone sales or software development, but a good, old-fashioned occupation: hairdressing. The growth of the range of jobs across the service sector has been phenomenal.

Negotiating the 21st century career minefield

Moving beyond the boundaries

The growth of new kinds of work means that we cannot rely on inherited ideas about career choice, about where the safe jobs are, or even make decisions based on the career choices of the previous generation.

Shifting sands

The rapidly changing workplace means that it's very difficult to predict which industries may experience future skills shortages. By the time you are mid-career, your chosen occupation may have changed beyond recognition.

Learning new thinking skills

We need to know more about what's out there, but most of all we need to learn how to think differently. This means taking to idea building as a learned discipline. Very few people learn how to rethink their career options creatively enough.

Resisting inherited clichés

Career development usually requires the ability to distinguish between market reality (which is rich and varied) and the kind of clichés about work that so often control us. Many of the ideas we use to shape our work strategy (e.g. 'become a specialist' or 'work hard and you'll make progress') are at least a generation out of date.

Negotiating for yourself

Many workers are trained in successful negotiation or the art of managing relationships. What very few do is learn how to apply these skills to their own careers.

BEGINNING TO TAKE CONTROL

We've looked at the rapidly changing face of work. Now it's

time to focus on the way you engage with your career and with the increasing range of choices open to you.

How passive is your career plan? How much does your future depend on the intervention of others – your boss, your colleagues, Human Resources? If your strategy is to sit tight, keep your head down and work hard, that might just work. Opportunities for growth, development, and variety *may* just come along. On the other hand, you're not doing much to improve the odds. Being passive about our career futures is a tried and tested model, and you may be put under some pressure to conform to it: *don't rock the boat, don't draw attention to yourself, just keep your head down* .... .

The passive model is the one we inherited from a time when employers did your career thinking for you: organized your training, planned your promotion steps, looked after your interest. Sixty years ago the idea that you had any real influence over your career, working hours, conditions or duties was completely alien to Western culture. You did the job, and you worked through until you got a pension. Employers essentially offered workers a 'deal' – give us your hard work and your loyalty, and we'll give you job security and a future. This 'psychological contract' broke down somewhere in the 1990s after countless rounds of downsizing, 'rightsizing', and restructuring.

Bill worked for a water board as a surveyor. He enjoyed some aspects of the job, but felt he was over-qualified for the role. Occasionally more senior jobs became vacant, but after being turned down for one he was reluctant to press any further. If they want me for the job they'll invite me to apply, he thought. Finally a career step came in sight: his boss's retirement, 5 years away. All Bill had to do was work hard and wait for the job to fall into his lap. Twelve months before his boss's retirement day the unit was privatized. Bill was made redundant after his post was contracted out.

Two generations ago only a minority really thought they had any kind of career choices, and an even smaller percentage of workers believed they could make decisions or take steps that would turn choices into actions. So the idea that you can take control of your career is relatively new. But it's one of the most powerful ideas around – one that will have as much impact on your personal fulfilment and happiness as any other life choice.

What kind of choices?

You may be looking for the next, obvious step up the ladder. You may be looking for a sideways move. You may be looking for tools to help you renegotiate your role with your organization. You may feel that work absorbs too much of you, and you're looking to make a change in your life/work balance.

It's Sunday night and a working week awaits you. Do you go to bed depressed, or looking forward to the excitement of the tasks ahead? Does anticipating the week ahead fill you with dread, with apathetic acceptance, or with energy? What really motivates you to set your alarm clock for a dark and icy January morning? And why do you sit there week after week doing work that doesn't matter to you, and uses only a fraction of your skills?

Being in control of your career means different things to different people. It isn't just thinking about your next step up the ladder. For some people it's about finding a way to continue learning. For others it's about achieving recognition. For some it's about moving into a job that is more interesting and fulfilling. It's about being stretched. To achieve that, you have to know what kind of work is right for you in the future. **Table 1.1** discusses some of the options for taking control of your career. How many of them have you *really* considered?

Table 1.1 Starting to look at career choice

Options	Key thinking
Seeking your first position	The hardest thing near the beginning of your career is that many jobs look the same. It's important to gain varied experience quickly. Investigate the options available to you, and look particularly closely at the career pathways that will open up to you through your learning opportunities.
Moving on from an entry level position	Be flexible, learn quickly, then ask for new tasks and responsibilities. Show interest, energy, and a hunger to learn, and at the same time don't neglect your present job. Ask about the minimum entry standards for the next role, and how much flexibility there is around qualifications or experience.
Moving from a temporary or contract post to a permanent position	You have a great chance of doing this just by sticking around, getting to know the right people, showing motivation and interest, and by looking and sounding just like someone who already works there.
Continuing along the learning curve	Do you feel you're not learning any more? Feeling under-challenged? Time to make sure you are availing yourself of the full range of training available to you, or seek on the job training and work experience. What can you learn outside the job?
Influencing your employer to create a new job around you	Don't be put off by company rules and the way things are normally done. Companies break promotion rules all the time to get the right results. This is far more likely than you think. Begin by taking on projects where you can demonstrate initiative and achieve results

Continued

	quickly. Most importantly, don't neglect to ask for the opportunity, no matter how ambitious. Seek out clear opportunities to match your employer's Key Result Areas (see **Chapter 5**).
Moving into the next grade up from your present level	What know-how do you need to demonstrate to be considered suitable for this role? If there are company rules and expectations about time served, age, or experience, actively seek out examples where these rules have been bent.
Achieving a significant promotion	Again, look for examples where others have done this before you. What skills or specialist knowledge did they demonstrate? How did they behave? How were they seen by the organization? Seek opportunities to train, develop and monitor other members of staff to indicate your management potential.
Changing direction	Track down pathfinders: people who have moved on from your present occupation. Talk to them about the strategies they used. Invest time in discovery, focusing on conversations with real people rather than documentary evidence.
Taking a career break	Again, find people who have done it before you before exploring whether your organization will tolerate or even support such a move. Think carefully about how you will fund the break, and what you will say about it in your CV and at interview when you return to the job market.
Finding a better balance	Do you keep making promises to yourself or those close to you that you don't keep? This is usually a strong indicator that you might want to look at the way you spend your time and energy, using tools such as the one in **Chapter 8** to assist.

Complete the questionnai

Book your <u>free</u> appointment NOW
Snow Hill, Wolverha

CASCAiD **Adult Directions**

You can enter Skills (from work, hom
life or hobbies) and Adult Directions
will use them in the career matching.

Book Your
Appointment Today!

scover your perfect career!

floor reception at Central Library,
r call 01902 552026.

Adult Directions ▾

Welcome to Adult Directions

ow can we help you today?

ant to find a career based on my "Likes & slikes" ❯

ant to find a career based on my "Skills" ❯

ant to find a career based on both my "Likes & slikes" and my "Skills" ❯

ave a career idea of my own ❯

ant to plan my career path ❯

ant to browse the Information Library ❯

EXERCISE 1.1 – AUDITING YOUR PRESENT ROLE

Usually the best place to begin to take control is to learn how to look at your present role with improved perspective. We start by analysing the overall fit of your job. Which areas of your job don't cut it for you? What do you really enjoy about your present role? Complete the audit in Table 1.2.

Table 1.2 Auditing Your Present Role

Place an appropriate score on each line

Negative characteristics	
This description is true ...	Most of the time 3 points Some of the time 2 points Hardly ever 1 point Not at all 0 points
1 I am underemployed	
2 I am not using my skills	
3 I am not learning new skills	
4 The job doesn't challenge me	
5 I feel uncomfortable with the people I work alongside	
6 I dislike the way I am managed	
7 I dislike the way things are done at work	
8 I feel trapped in the job	
9 I feel I have very different values to my employer/others at work	
10 I feel undervalued at work	
11 I feel like calling in sick or avoiding work	
12 I complain about my job	
Total negative score	

Positive characteristics		
This description is true …	Most of the time	3 points
	Some of the time	2 points
	Hardly ever	1 point
	Not at all	0 points
13 I have fun at work		
14 Work is interesting and absorbing		
15 I feel I would do the same job for half the money		
16 The job has variety		
17 I enjoy working with the people around me		
18 I have some influence over outcomes or the way things are done		
19 I feel I make a difference		
20 I feel my role is a very good match to my skills		
21 My boss delegates to my strengths		
22 I have a sense of progress in the job		
23 I have a chance to learn new ideas, techniques or skills		
24 I talk positively to my friends about my job		
Total positive score		

Look at your results from **Table 1.2**. A role that is a good match to your interests and personality is likely to give you a positive score 10–15 points higher than your negatives. If your overall score is positive, you have a great starting point for career enhancement because you will be building on a role that meets many of your drivers. If you are scoring more than 25 or so on your negatives, clearly you need to begin to take control fairly quickly. The good news is that you can do a huge amount for yourself by taking active control – and it doesn't automatically have to mean changing jobs.

Olivia has been temping in her organization for 4 months. She feels underemployed. She can see people with poorer qualifications than hers enjoying well-paid roles. On the verge of asking for an assignment somewhere else, Olivia was offered a choice: do nothing and stay as a temp, or move to another organization, or actively seek help. She chose the last choice, seeking a meeting with her line manager. She was surprised to hear that she was a valued member of the team, and that she had introduced several new ideas that had improved systems in the organization. Furthermore, although this employer doesn't normally offer career development support for temps, in this case it was prepared to re-invent the rules. She now has several internal meetings lined up with managers, first to find out more about the organization, and secondly to investigate the possibility of permanent jobs.

'MUST DO': YOUR 10 FIRST STEPS FOR TAKING CONTROL

1. Look at the positives and negatives in your present role using **Exercise 1.1**.

2. What can you change quickly? What can you change in the long term?

3. What should your new role feel like in terms of work satisfaction?

4. Write a detailed picture of your ideal job (boss, team, problems, opportunities, work environment, skills).

5. Write down your answer to the question: *'What benefits do I bring to my job?'*

6. How would your employer answer the same question?

7. Start putting together a folder of documents that records where you have added valued or made a difference.

8. Talk to others in the organization about the jobs they do: find out the people and the activities that really shape outcomes.

9. Seek out pathfinders: people who have taken your chosen path before you. Learn from their mistakes, and from their enthusiasm.

10. Perform a quick energy audit: how much time do you really have left at the end of a working week for the things you feel are important in life?

What Makes a Career Come Together?

This chapter helps you to:

▌ Understand how others achieve career enhancement

▌ Spot the pitfalls on the way

▌ Gain insights into how people achieve above-average career progression

▌ Identify attitudes and behaviours that encourage employers to value you

▌ Identify signposts to success

Work as if you'd been already promoted.

Daniel Porot

Before you learn to take control, let's take a few moments to learn from others who have been there before you.

This chapter takes an in-depth look at the results of a survey that examines how and why people are successful in their careers. The survey was conducted among a wide range of business professionals, all of them people established in their careers. Many respondents are now in senior positions or running their own businesses, but most importantly they are all people who have taken steps to exert some kind of control over their career pathway. Respondents are from the UK,

Ireland, the USA, Canada, Spain, Germany, Switzerland, and South Africa. What they all have in common is significant business and management expertise, plus an insight into the way their careers developed. The respondents in the survey have a combined total of about 1,750 years of work experience and wisdom.

What makes some careers come together? You'll notice that the question asked here isn't about success – financial or otherwise. Nor is it a matter of whether or not you achieve promotion. A career 'comes together' when what we do for a living aligns with the deeper things we want to get out of life. Sometimes that occurs by chance, but usually we have to do something to make it happen. Some people do this instinctively and call it luck. The majority of us have a choice between passive acceptance of a career that is influenced by external, random factors, or something we choose for ourselves.

SURVEY QUESTIONS

The survey asked questions around these key areas:

- Key actions or events identified as formative steps in building a career.

- The best approaches and strategies to achieve career development and success.

- What steps individuals have taken to take control of their careers.

- The actions taken to put careers in balance with other commitments.

- The specific behaviours and attitudes which lead to career progression.

- What single piece of advice would you give to someone who wants to achieve a promotion at work in the next 12 months?

KEY ACTIONS OR EVENTS IDENTIFIED AS FORMATIVE STEPS

When asked about key actions and events, the top three areas of feedback were as follows:

1. Self-awareness.

2. Finding a mentor or sponsor.

3. Returning to full-time study or education.

Self-awareness

Several respondents gave an answer that describes a moment when their self-awareness increased significantly: a new realization about themselves and their abilities, their role or their employer. For some, this was a realization of what they didn't like doing, and a realization that they were spending too much time doing things they found unrewarding.

Claire Coldwell, career coach and UK President of the Association of Career Professionals International, sums this up as knowing yourself, and knowing what the industry needs: 'If you're aware of your strengths and weaknesses and you understand how other see you, and you can maximize the former and develop the latter to address the issues which you see the industry is facing, then you'll be ahead of the game. Both of these require some effort, but if you enjoy your job, that's not too difficult.'

One manager simply answered: 'awareness of company unwritten codes and cultures and working to them'. The emphasis is on the *unwritten* aspect – learning to switch on your radar to work out what really is going on in an organization.

For many, self-awareness led to critical action. Typical steps included some way of negotiating a move into an exciting role or project. Some found that short-term roles (e.g. covering for illness or maternity leave) opened opportunities. Others took a more proactive approach. Alan Small, while working as a product manager in a large multinational, transformed the way that his company saw him when he challenged the results of his annual appraisal that damned him with faint praise: 'I insisted on getting clarification on the criteria used in judging me and was given a month to demonstrate that the view of me in the appraisal was not valid. (This happens frequently with quiet people, where 'quiet' is taken to be the same as 'soft'. I had to persuade my masters that 'firm' was every bit as effective as 'loud' and often much more acceptable).'

Carole Pemberton, author and founder of Career Matters, believes that 'For me achieving self-awareness has been the key to making career decisions that are right for each phase of my life.' She uses a striking image: 'My career has built like a spiral but held together by a firm core. Significant actions only seem significant in retrospect, but to me the starting point was when I started to listen to myself rather than worrying about what I ought to do. I came to work with very few models to draw on – my family did not "do" careers, they simply had jobs.' Ultimately she believes that career building has 'come from combining the desire to develop my learning and the willingness to take a risk – to step away from what I have become comfortable with. The risks have never seemed like risks because the centre of the spiral has always given me a sense that I am taking important parts of me into the new situation.'

Finding a mentor or sponsor

An almost universal comment was the need to have a supportive network. For some this was about enlisting senior and influential figures who can champion your case. Having friends, family, or colleagues who were prepared to listen was also important, particularly if they are the kind of people who believe in you.

Many feel it vital to gain 'sponsorship', that is, active support from a senior staff members. This may be a formal mentor, or (more likely), someone more experienced than you who values your contribution and wants to help you find a safe path through the organizational minefield. David Podger, Commercial Director of Hawksmere Ltd, adds: 'Don't confine those mentors to people who have business or professional experience – some of the best advice I have had has come from exceptional people in completely unrelated fields.'

Networking is seen as most helpful with people that have influence and can make decisions, but it's important to demonstrate that you can get on with anyone you work with. Sometimes it helps to identify sponsors who are seeking career advancement for themselves, and then proving to them that you are worthy of their support. A word of caution: when your mentor leaves, you may hit a career block.

NHS Executive Val Michej insists that you 'Don't expect anyone else to manage your career development or create opportunities for you, because you may wait forever. Do it yourself and do it for yourself, never for anyone else. If you do find someone who actively supports you, regard it as a bonus – and then treasure them forever!'

Returning to full-time study or education

A number of respondents made a significant change to their careers by going back into education. In some instances a specific qualification was required to make a job move, but for many education had a powerful and unexpected effect: broadening horizons. The important thing is to focus on learning (see **Chapter 8** to help you understand your personal learning curve).

Others found ways of learning by taking on additional responsibilities. Canadian outplacement specialist Garth Toombs saw learning a key to building his career: 'leaving a job was often stimulated by feeling I had gone as far as I could or wanted to in the role'.

Other key events or decisions included:

I Understanding and achieving corporate goals (see **Chapter 5** for far more on this topic).

I Applying for promotion.

I Moving and gaining experience in a variety of businesses, but also being prepared to relocate and live in different countries.

I Being prepared to take a risk, e.g. self-funding a plane ticket to USA for a job interview, or leaving a secure job to start a new business.

I For some respondents personal turning points such as ill health brought about a realignment of career values.

APPROACHES AND STRATEGIES TO ACHIEVE CAREER DEVELOPMENT AND SUCCESS

When asked about taking control of their own career development, the majority of respondents talked about using a combination of different strategies. For example, Human Resources consultant Anne Stojic: 'I believe the key is to build relationships and make an impression with the right people ... However I would also say it is important to anticipate what skills/experiences are required for the next promotion and work towards these in advance. In the past I have asked to attend training courses and also asked for extra responsibilities at work, this way before long you are doing a higher level job anyway.'

Career progression is also tied up with raising your profile. Two respondents tell us that the key event for them was applying for promotion but being unsuccessful. However, in making the application, they both raised their profile so that they were either headhunted, or considered for the next post. One respondent highlighted that it was only when goals and delivery requirements were confirmed in writing with her CEO that she achieved her promotion.

The most frequent responses can be summarized under the following five headings:

1. Working hard and doing a good job.

2. Making the best and most visible impact in your organization.

3. Working upwards.

4. Understanding organizational politics.

5. Understanding and achieving company goals.

Working hard and doing a good job

'Doing a good job' may be the nation's favourite career strategy, but respondents were keen to emphasize the need to move beyond your job description, going the extra mile by what one respondent called 'being the solution rather than the problem'.

It's vital to have a clear understanding of your job: 'Know your company, its products/services, your colleagues and do your job particularly well', stated Rod Howgate, founding partner of recruitment consultancy Howgate Sable. 'Demonstrate a little more commitment than that portrayed by those peers around you', suggests Communications Director Mike Wallwork.

Keep learning about your organization's needs by focusing on the jobs other people do: 'Talk to people in different jobs to ensure you know what they entail', suggests Rob Head. 'Find out what these jobs need and if you could make an impression by doing them. *Never* choose a job because it sounds important – you must be able to do well in it.'

Sally Skidmore, Career Consultant with J.P. Morgan Chase in New York, suggests: 'Align yourself with those with similar work and career success values. Take the initiative in all you do: ideas, actions, interpersonal relationships, and projects. Learn to work collaboratively with open and inclusive communication and trust, keeping all parties well informed about the good and, where there are problems, offer solutions. Ask for new challenges and opportunities.'

Indeed, some respondents specifically mentioned that you should ensure that your superiors are kept informed and never surprised by events. **Chapter 10** tells you a lot more about managing your relationship with the boss. Find out what your boss is looking for when considering promoting someone, talk his or her language, and be aware of the talent that is available outside the organization.

Make the best and most visible impact in your organization

Working hard, even if it's on key objectives, may not be enough. You need to be noticed by the right people – the decision-makers: 'Apart from doing a good job and delivering results, it is making sure that someone (preferably as many as possible) in a position of influence knows it' (Outplacement consultant Bill Hollyhead).

Most responses under this heading suggest that you identify what the business needs, move into that area, and focus your attention only on the points where visible impact can be achieved. Often this means building relationships with those who can help you do what you do best, and finding opportunities for exposure in your areas of competence.

Founder and MD of Career Management Consultants Limited (CMC), Robin Wood, states: 'be seen to put the company's needs first, volunteering for assignments and projects and then working like hell in a highly visible manner to deliver.'

Being visible is a subtle task, and is about both reality and perception. The reality may be that you're under-stimulated by your present role. However, your manager may have a completely different picture, thinking that you're happy doing what you are doing, and the best strategy is to leave you alone. Even worse, you may have made some mistakes recently because you no longer find the role demands your full attention. Your manager may read the mistakes as 'underperforming' rather than 'losing interest because the job is over-familiar'. Deirdre Hughes Director, Centre for Guidance Studies at the University of Derby, writes of the importance of 'being willing to analyse situations from differing perspectives and being prepared to find ways in which your line managers feel you are working "with" them rather than "against" them. Sometimes this means having to let go and helping them think through ideas to find the appropriate answers for themselves (supported by evidence, guidance and advice that you can feed into the process!).'

Having good personal qualities was seen as key by many people: 'be professional in all that you do and become the kind of person people can trust and rely on. Don't undermine others, give credit where it's due' (Careers coach Rob Stickland). Mike Wallwork cited that it was important to 'have opinions and your own mind. Most people seem to respond more favourably to those that have an opinion than those that follow other "corporate" views.'

It is important to be noticed for the right reasons. Positive incidents can create opportunities, negative events can block you for years. Garth Toombs recalls that one manager in a major corporation was 'let go' because of an incident that had happened 10 years earlier when this employee had been inebriated at a company party and had been rude to the president's wife.

Working upwards

Working upwards is, essentially, identifying the skills and experience that are required for the next level up and actively building them into your CV: 'I took to noting those qualities in those above me which make them particularly good either in their job or as leaders. I then sought to emulate them, wherever possible, and without aping them, did what they were doing, only better' (RAF selector Keith Harden). Life Coach Beverley Gartside suggests that 'it helps if you are already seen to be operating at the level to which you aspire'.

Keeping your eyes and ears open to opportunities was seen as very important: 'try to avoid saying "no" to good opportunities, recognizing that you can usually negotiate on any unsatisfactory elements of roles and jobs' (John Eardley).

Linda Walmsley, executive recruiter and former newspaper advertising executive, found it useful 'offering to help with anything else that was going on in the department. Two benefits – I really enjoyed learning about someone else's role and pressures and they had more time for me in my current job because I had given them some help.'

One response suggested that if you are going to make yourself indispensable, do so by demonstrating general transferable skills rather than skills restricted to particular job, as you may get stuck there.

'Don't think of promotion as the target', suggests outplacement specialist Ron Feasey. For him the question is rather 'How can I make a bigger contribution to the organization and/or how can I widen my experience? Overt career ambition can turn off managers.'

Understanding organizational politics

More than a few respondents made comments on the importance of being aware of organizational politics, and knowing how to handle the odd bout of back stabbing. Some suggest explicitly that you should work the system by identifying the people who have power and influence in the organization, and find out how they can be influenced. One respondent writes cynically: 'The guys at the top didn't get here by being wholly good at their jobs, they have climbed there on the backs of their fallen colleagues. These guys are mostly driven people who see the world with different eyes from their normal colleagues. If you are not a driven guy don't bother entering the race! Find a senior manager who thinks you are good and let him drag you through.'

It's also important to know that sometimes you can't beat the system and therefore you need to divert your energies elsewhere. The issue of organizational politics is discussed in depth in **Chapter 7**.

Learn a critical skill: how to handle your boss (see **Chapter 10** for more on this topic). Executive recruiter Joëlle Warren: 'Learn to manage your boss, make your boss look good to their boss'. At times this is about understanding and building on your boss's motivations of fear and greed: 'Make your boss think they are vulnerable because you are about to go somewhere else. Alternatively, deliver something so valuable to them that they put themselves in a difficult position if they don't promote you' wryly suggests consumer marketing expert Philip Spencer.

Understanding and achieving company goals

This was seen as key to a number of respondents, and so gets special focus in **Chapter 5**. Coaching specialist Stuart Carter writes: 'Focus on key drivers that you can influence and will directly link to the senior people you aspire to join, e.g. customer satisfaction, sales targets, revenue and cost reduction.'

Overall, there's much to be said for managing critical relationships with people who have a big say in your future.

Fred Mahoney, who has spent many years managing companies in the UK and USA, says that you should 'Analyse and identify the characteristics of the managers promoted to senior positions in the company you work for. If the company promotes commodity traders to senior positions and you are a technical manager then the chances are that you will not be promoted ... in most corporations there are glass ceilings through which you cannot pass unless you have certain characteristics.' Occasionally these characteristics may not be related in any real way to an individual's ability to do the job.

Other successful strategies aimed at career progression included:

I Having a clear notion of where you want to go, understanding your life's priorities and taking steps to move in that direction.

I Being thoroughly prepared for appraisals.

I Be careful not to accept a promotion or transfer uncritically – look at what you're letting yourself in for.

I Be prepared to move – in some organizations this means the readiness to work anywhere and with anyone. This may be a matter of moving to the heart of the action, e.g. to head office.

I Developing subordinates so that you have someone ready to take over your position.

I Telling your managers about your ambitions. Don't wait passively for someone to spot your talent – you may wait forever.

HOW YOU BEGIN TO TAKE CONTROL

Career coach Derek Osborn, formerly a senior operational manager with the Post Office, identified the moment when he saw the need to move from passive to active mode: 'I needed to take control of my career and not wait for my boat to come in – rather swim out to it.'

David Podger writes: 'I make a plan – and set annual dates for review. I try to take it seriously, if necessarily I make an appointment with someone who can help me. Just having the structure in place gives me the sense that I'm managing my future.'

Writer Maureen Rice-Knight talks about breaking away from the constraints of the organization. She recalls her career as a staff journalist, progressing 'in a conventional way from junior to department head to editor. My success up to this point was largely due to blending in. I'm not being disingenuous: I was good at my job and delivered good results. But I also played the company game. I didn't rock the boat, or tread on anybody's toes. It worked up to a point, but the action which really helped me progress – both professionally and personally – was leaving the long-term security of my job to go freelance. Outside a corporate structure I became both braver and more honest about who and I what I really am. My ideas became better and my delivery of them – now that I was genuinely invested in them as *my* ideas – became far more creative and effective. It was the single best move I ever made in my life.'

Taking control without putting your career out of balance

It's easy to think about career development as being a simple matter of moving up the career ladder.

Progression often has a cost – in terms of time, and personal energy. The more reflective respondents to our survey indicated ways in which they had try to extend their self-awareness to an understanding of the way their work impacted on their health, personal relationships, and sense of fulfilment. Maureen Rice-Knight suggests: 'Don't focus on the promotion. Focus on engaging with some aspect of your work where you can bring yourself to it. Inevitably, this is how you'll be at your best.'

Several responses focused on the importance of maintaining work/life balance, for example Joëlle Warren: 'Don't win in business and lose in life – your family and friends deserve more than what left after you've give your best to your work and they'll still be there when the job's gone.'

Julia Robertson, MD of Carlisle Staffing Services, has similar advice: 'Be very clear on why your are doing this, what you will bring to the new position and how you would benefit the company in the role. Don't forget how this new position will impact on your personal life (bring loved ones on board). Be aware that a position of responsibility may be isolating and distance you from some former friends. Are you ready for this?'

Finding and maintaining the right balance between working and living is essential in taking control of your career – so much so that a great deal of **Chapter 8** is dedicated to the issue.

SPECIFIC BEHAVIOURS AND ATTITUDES THAT LEAD TO CAREER PROGRESSION

Approaches and strategies (i.e. how you bring your skills, personality and attitudes into play) really matter. Most people felt that both attitudes and observable behaviours are vital. Key attitudes to being seen as promotable material are:

▮ Demonstrating a high level of commitment to the company.

▮ Being solutions not problem focused.

▮ Having a 'can-do' attitude.

▮ Demonstrating enthusiasm.

▮ Showing integrity.

▮ Being respected.

▮ Being willing make personal sacrifices.

This research is supported by those experienced in recruitment. There is often a big difference between a job description and the real factors that determine success in a role. A job description often focuses on tasks, skills, and responsibilities (in other words, behaviours). However, ask a senior manager what *really* makes a successful post holder and the answer will usually be about attitudes and style. (This is, of course, one of the principles behind competency-based recruitment, since a competence is not just what you can do, but how you do it; competencies are defined by looking at the skills, behaviours, know-how, values, and attitudes of top performers.) The broad lesson is that to progress in your career you need not just to possess certain qualities, but find ways of communicating them as observed behaviours. You also need to find some way of incorporating them into active approaches and strategies.

A number of respondents stated that the answer to the above question depended on the culture of the company. It's important to interpret and match the style of senior managers and to echo the company's values.

WHAT SINGLE PIECE OF ADVICE WOULD YOU GIVE TO SOMEONE WHO WANTS TO ACHIEVE A PROMOTION AT WORK IN THE NEXT 12 MONTHS?

The primary responses to this question are summarized in **Table 2.1**. Further ideas and strategies are rehearsed in **Chapters 12** and **13**.

Table 2.1 Advice for the next 12 months

▪ Be clear on what you want: have a plan of action and stick to it

▪ Know the business and where you can make the best visible impact

▪ Identify key decision-makers and network

▪ Raise your profile

▪ Be flexible and realistic

▪ Do a good job, exceed expectations, focus on your self-development

Continued

I Know the way the company works (and work that way)

I Develop strong teamwork skills

I Know which battles are worth fighting in the short term

I Don't be afraid to have a view and to express your own opinions

I Develop a strong ability to think and plan ahead

I Be a generalist rather than a specialist

I Show your ability to see the big picture (and work towards it)

I Demonstrate idea-building and innovation

I Learn how to manage change in yourself and others

I Learn how to be resilient!

Knowing what you want

Our survey reinforces the idea that it's considered important to be clear about what you want, have an overall game plan, and communicate it. Derek Osborn advises: 'First work out what exact job or role you want so that you can be very goal focused. A general wish for promotion is likely to be less successful as you will not get through the selection process without a very clear idea of why you want the promotion.'

'Ask yourself why you want the promotion,' says David Podger, 'is it for more money, or are you simply chasing a different job title, or is it really because you want a change of role and wider responsibilities? Are you prepared to move outside your comfort zone and move into a different area? If so, explore the possibility of using your skills in a different setting within the same organization. Use your imagination: promotion means moving upwards, but that can be diagonally as well as vertically.'

Stuart McIntosh, Managing Consultant for Career Management Consultants Ltd, pushes you to ask deeper questions: 'Is the next step in your career right for you? Have you looked externally in order to benchmark? Do you have short-, medium- and long-term goals in your career and personally?'

Jo Bond, UK Managing Director of outplacement specialists Right Coutts, has a short and sharp piece of advice on promotion: 'Ask for it! Make sure that those with the power to grant your wish know that you want it!'

And if your attempt to gain promotion doesn't work?

Here the voice of experience suggests that you need to be aware when you are flogging a dead horse. Knowing when your strategy isn't working is about understanding when it may be time to jump ship. **Chapter 11** offers guidance on knowing when you've reached this point, and how to plan your departure carefully.

Equally, don't rigid a time limit on gaining promotion. Jane Moorhouse believes that 'if there is nowhere for you to be promoted then work at improving your skill base'.

'MUST DO' LIST

☑ What one key action or event has helped you in your career? How can you repeat that step, or build on it?

☑ What strategies or approaches outlined here can help you succeed?

☑ What behaviours/ attitudes/ approaches have you used effectively at work?

☑ Which do you need to develop?

☑ How are you going to build on the advice you have been given about taking action within the next 12 months? (See also **Chapter 13** for further tips.)

Becoming Your Own Career Pilot

CHAPTER 3

This chapter helps you to:

▌ Rethink the idea of your career

▌ Adopt a 'career awareness' strategy

▌ Check the main focus of your work

▌ Learn how to be your own career coach

▌ Conduct your own six-step career review

We do not deal much in facts when we are contemplating ourselves.

Mark Twain

WHERE TO BEGIN

Having looked at how others have managed their careers in **Chapter 2**, we now move to active steps you can follow. This begins with a DIY career review – becoming your own career coach.

Undertaking a personal review is one of those activities we're happy to put off – like dental flossing or throwing out old photographs. Both analogies are useful. First of all, we need to think about how healthy our jobs are at present, and what maintenance we need to do. Secondly, from time to time we need to review our past – just like pulling out an old photograph album.

When a large ship approaches harbour it picks up a pilot – a trained officer who knows the local waters well. No matter how senior the captain of the ship, command shifts to an outsider during a few critical manoeuvres. We can do the same thing in our careers. We turn to mentors, experienced friends or advisers. We put our careers in the hands of human resources departments or managers. We sit back and watch them pilot us around the breakwater and into harbour, relieved to get safely alongside.

That's the model most of us have inherited as far as job progress is concerned. We entrust it to others: we hope our line manager will notice the contribution we've made; we hope that a successful appraisal may mean that the boss keeps us in mind for more interesting work. Some of these strategies may work, but they all rely too much on other people.

DIY piloting makes you master of your own ship. *You* make the critical steps, you begin to shape your future around the kind of work you find satisfying and motivating. Most importantly of all, *you* decide when, where, and how.

When should you conduct your career review?

Ideally you should do some kind of career review activity every 3 months, even if this is only keeping a record of your successes, and adding to your networking. Other critical times will be:

▌ When you're in a fast-moving environment and opportunities are throwing themselves at you day by day.

▌ When you feel you have more to offer your organization.

▌ When things are going well and you want to build on success.

▌ When you're applying for a new position or a promotion.

▌ When you feel you've learned all there is to learn in your job.

▌ When you're unhappy in your work and want to change something.

Can you really control your career? This is a question I am asked all the time by workshop delegates, and yet there is evidence all around us that DIY career management is increasingly possible and necessary. Perhaps we don't recognize when other people achieve it. More likely, we assume this is something only other people do.

Rethink 'career'

The whole idea of a 'career' has undergone huge changes over the past two generations. We're all familiar with the idea that none of us has a job for life. We know that it's very likely that we will have to change jobs and possibly even careers. So we feel that we should do some 'career planning'. However this seems like a very demanding mix of hard work and future gazing.

We all feel everyone else has a career plan. In fact, very few people have their lives planned out that precisely. Even so, we feel guilty for letting our working lives be guided by chance – the job that just happens to come along. It's as if you are going to plan a holiday by picking on the first flight you find on the airport departures board. A great strategy for a spontaneous adventure, but perhaps not the best way of deciding how to spend 100,000 hours of your waking life.

Beware the idea of the perfect job

It's important to dispel the myth of the perfect job. You can hear people talking about what they would do 'in an ideal world'. The danger with the idea of the perfect job, a job that provides 100% satisfaction, is that we know that perfection never comes along – most jobs have a downside. And once we believe that

that, we set up a false choice: ideal job, or real world. We use the idea of the perfect job to avoid getting a better job – in fact to avoid doing anything.

You don't have to get the perfect job, or a job that you will love all the time. However, you might like to consider an idea that you can do something about: *making your job better than it is*. The chances are that even if promotion isn't your explicit goal, this will probably happen as a result of the attention you give to role development. People take what you do more seriously when you focus on the things you do well and communicate your successes.

If you genuinely cannot improve the job you're in, then career development will be about moving towards a job (or an organization, or a lifestyle) that is a much better match for you.

LEARNING THE ART OF 'CAREER AWARENESS'

Career awareness is an antidote to traditional ideas about career planning. Career awareness is not about having a cast-iron 20-year career plan, but an ability to rapidly match opportunity to personal goals. For some people it will also be about the long game – the kind of role you want to hold in 5–10 years' time. For most of us, it's about being alert *now*. It's a strategy that doesn't depend on luck or job change, but begins with three basic questions:

▪ What kind of work do I really want to do?

▪ What does my employer really need?

▪ How can I exploit the overlap, or create one?

This strategy avoids the pitfalls of long-term career planning and focuses on both quick wins: positioning yourself for changes you can make in your career within the next 6–12 months. Secondly, the emphasis is very much on what you have to offer now, rather than falling back on the idea that you have to retrain or go back to full-time education (again, two great reasons to put off career development).

What kind of awareness is involved? Awareness of yourself, how others see you (see more about personality later in this chapter), awareness of what your present or future employer is really looking for, and an understanding of the way work is changing.

Sandy was temping for a major UK organization concerned with culture and the arts. She originally took the job just to do secretarial work, but gradually discovered that the organization has many overlaps with her personal areas of interest: culture, languages, foreign travel, project management.

Even as a temp she has been allowed to benefit from company training programmes. Having enlisted the support of her line manager, Sandy took every opportunity she could to meet people from different departments of the organization, to discover what roles are available, and to undertake suitable training. She has also re-affirmed her project management and team skills, and currently presents a positive message that will make her a highly suitable candidate when permanent vacancies occur within the organization.

What is your focus?

In a world where technical skills are being taken for granted, there is increasingly more attention to interpersonal skills, and how you use them. The business environment changes very fast, and a highly valued staff don't just to ride the wave of change, but keep ahead of it. Being focused means knowing what you're good at, and being able to communicate that to decision-makers – your present boss, other managers in the organization, and not forgetting representatives of outside organizations including customers. 'Be the best you can be at what you do', suggests Californian career coach Carla Barrett: 'Receive good training and continue to learn new things every year'.

Your career focus needs to be about *how* you handle this week's problems, and how far others are aware of your results. If multi-tasking and managing complex problems comes easily, perhaps your contribution is undervalued because you don't value your skills and accomplishments. It's important that people who will have a say in your future have a sense of what you *really* do – the times when you have snatched victory from the jaws of defeat, the times when a calming influence rescued a key account, or a clear head made a key event run smoothly.

Your contribution matters to the bottom line of your business and to the peace of mind of your boss. But be aware that your duties include a responsibility to yourself to make sure the way you execute your role is appreciated.

DIY CAREER PILOTING

Time to move away from being inactive ('next year I'll make time to review my career properly') or passive ('who can help find me another job?'). Time to take control. You can do this by learning from the way others have managed their careers (see **Chapter 2** and elsewhere), but also by learning how to use some of the techniques a career coach would use with you.

The benefits of DIY career piloting

Time to take your first tentative steps towards coaching yourself towards success. Becoming the pilot of your own future means that you begin to learn:

■ how to tell the difference between what you can fix, and what you can't

■ how to obtain and exert leverage

■ how you can make a difference or add value

■ how being in the right place at the right time is no mere coincidence

■ how to manage your luck

■ how to make decisions, rather than be subject to them

■ how to recruit others to help you along the way.

DIY career review

You can't know where you're going unless you know where you've been. You can begin by looking at your past successes (and not quite successes). In **Chapter 1** you had an opportunity to conduct an audit of your job satisfaction. That's the first step. Take stock of what you've done and what you have to offer by working through the following six stages of your DIY career review:

A   diagnose your constraints

B   formulate your goals and message

C   identify your skills and achievements

D   realize your intellectual capital

E   understand the way your personality fits into work

F   examine your attitudes and values.

A. Diagnose your constraints

Look at the pluses and minuses in your job, and take a positive look at both. How can you improve the good parts of the job? How can you diminish, delegate or avoid the uninspiring parts?

Most people don't find it difficult to list the problems in their jobs. However, as soon as the conversation turns to fixing them, we become highly creative at coming up with reasons why nothing can be done. Constraints are the barriers between you and success. Being a DIY coach is about really asking how far you are limited by external constraints, and how far internal blocks are getting in the way. **Table 3.1** shows you examples of both. Add your own at the end.

Table 3.1 Constraints

External constraints	Internal constraints
Can you get round them? If not, what's the best career strategy to work with them?	*Look at how far these prevent you from changing anything. Where have you overcome these problems in the past?*
Need to work near home	I'm under-qualified
I need to avoid a long commute	I'm too old
I want to live near where I work	I am no good at networking
Don't want to move house	I'm frightened of making the wrong move
I need £xxxx a month minimum	I'm not good at pushing myself forward
I have health problems or a disability	I hate being rejected
I have personal or family commitments	I'm frightened of losing my job

As **Table 3.1** reveals, we do have genuine constraints, but the most powerful ones are usually internal: the messages that keep you awake at two o'clock in the morning. These have a powerful effect on your *world view* – your picture of how life operates. Dealing with these constraints is vital as the first step in your DIY career review.

B. Formulate your goals and message

Chapter 4 tells you more about distinguishing goals from dreams. Work out the things that are real goals rather than unattainable fantasies.

With a goal in mind, you can build up a clear, coherent picture which combines your preferred skills, your intended pathways, and the kind of work you want to do. Your message may be communicated either verbally or in writing, but should be something you can condense into one sentence: *'I want my job to allow me to do A, B and C so that I (and my employer) can achieve X Y and Z.'*

Without making people bored or threatened, it's perfectly possible to let colleagues and managers know your message. Just be sure you offer it as a solution, not as a complaint (see **Chapter 10** for tips on offering a win/win 'deal').

You might like to give some thought to the question of when and how you communicate your message. With some people it will have an immediate impact and effect if you communicate verbally. You might then want to reinforce what you have said with an email or memo. Others take more time to respond, and don't accept new information readily. With this kind of manager or colleague it's often best to prime the pump by warning them that a piece of communication is on its way, and then sending something in writing. Indicate when you would like a follow-up discussion.

Think about what you may need to add to your message. Extraverts want to hear passion, logical people want to hear reasoning. Others want to see evidence, hear the benefits (*what's in it for me?*), or maybe want to see how what you suggest fits in to the big picture. Look at the communication strategies outlined in **Chapter 6**.

Ken is an associate with a specialist firm of consultants who advise businesses on cost reductions. He's felt stuck in his career for several years, and dissatisfied with his job. However in the past 12 months he has received two promotions. He had two turning points: one was to really look at his strengths, his achievements, and realize that he had far more to offer than his company was using. He drew up a strong CV, and developed a wish list of what he wanted to do next. The second change was a new boss. Instead of assuming the same kind of relationship with his new boss, Ken made a positive career pilot decision. He offered his new boss expertise and advice about getting the team to work better. He bought new suits and shirts. He put forward a range of initiatives that would present his boss 'quick wins' which would impress senior management. Now Ken gets taken along to the kind of meetings that only staff four rungs above him attend. Having a change of boss can sometimes mean you reposition yourself very astutely.

C. Identify your skills and achievements

The real key to getting your message straight is understanding what you are good at. This may seem perfectly obvious, but most recruiters will tell you that few candidates are fully aware of their skills, and fewer still are capable of communicating them – whether this is in a career review, an appraisal, or a job interview. Also, we good at complaining about the skills we are not allowed to use, but not so good at creating chances to do so. Most of us also need to find better ways to negotiate ways of improving skills or adding to our learning.

Career breakthrough requires you to know something about your *motivated skills* – those skills which you use competently *and* enjoy using. How do you recognize your motivated skills? The clues are fairly clear. When you use these skills, time seems to fly by. You become absorbed in the task at hand. You feel a sense of fulfilment in what you do, and the activity seems worth doing. It may even feel like fun. If this sounds unfamiliar, it could be that you haven't used your motivated skills at work for some time. Look at the things you choose to do when you are not in work, and you should see those skills fairly clearly.

However, do be aware that many of us fail to see our own skills simply because we have lived with them for so long. I call them 'wallpaper skills'. After your wallpaper has been up for a few months you no longer see it any more, at least until somebody comments on it, and then it snaps back into focus. Many of us use high-level interpersonal skills all the time, but we have stopped seeing them. Even when others point the skills out to us, we shrug them off. We often assume (quite wrongly) that everyone else has these skills.

Exercise 11.1 in **Chapter 11** provides a range of short cuts to skill identification.

D. Realize your intellectual capital

If you were only allowed to make a living from what you *know*, how would you set out your stall? Put another way, what specialist know-how, understanding or information do you have that makes you a key contributor to your organization? Employers are becoming increasingly concerned with the issue of knowledge retention – hanging on to the information, wisdom and contacts that we carry around in our heads and never record on paper or on disc. Often it's only when a member of staff leaves that managers discover the problem of missing knowledge. Therefore it makes sense to know what you know, and to think about how you can put others in the loop.

Your knowledge bank

▌ Topics on which colleagues have asked your advice.

▌ Areas of research, analysis, or surveys you have undertaken.

▌ Topics you have written reports on for internal use.

▌ Topics you have written articles on.

▌ Subjects you have trained others in, or spoken about at staff seminars.

▌ Areas of knowledge to which only a few individuals have access.

Extending your areas of knowledge

▌ Seek parallels from other industries or sectors.

▌ Find out how others achieve success and ask for their tips on shortcuts and minefields.

▌ Find out as much as you can about the work of others; become a fount of knowledge on who does what.

▌ Keep a cuttings file or resource book to record useful resources and contacts.

▌ Attend conferences and seminars, subscribe to e-groups – keep up to date with new ideas and approaches.

Showcasing your areas of knowledge

▌ Collect and distribute useful information.

▌ Ask to be given the chance to produce surveys of best practice, specialist techniques, or resources.

▌ Contribute to in-house or industry journals.

▌ Be known as an information broker: a great source of data and connections.

E. Understand the way your personality fits into work

If you want to move up in the organization, it pays to have an understanding of the way you relate to cultures and teams.

Find an opportunity to undertake some personality testing. What you should get is some helpful feedback about the way you respond in a variety of workplace situations. With some measures you will be given feedback around what psychologists call the 'big five' personality traits. One measure, **Quintax**, has been produced by Stuart Robertson & Associates in Manchester, UK (see www.sr-associates.com). Quintax's five-fold structure is outlined below as an example of the kind of feedback you will get from a well-developed personality measure.

1. **Extraversion**: this indicates whether you are more at home in the outer world of people and things, or in the inner world of ideas and reflection.

2. **Criticality**: this indicates whether you base your judgements more on impersonal logic and analysis or on personal values and feelings.

3. **Organization**: this concerns whether you like a decided and orderly way of dealing with life, or a more flexible spontaneous approach.

4. **Intellectual focus**: this is about whether you like to think about possibilities and relationships among ideas, or deal practically with known facts.

5. **Emotional involvement**: this describes whether you feel and express your emotions in reaction to events, or whether you tend to contain these reactions.

Each of these elements can help you to unlock the way your personality best integrates with different workplace situations. For example:

■ **Extraverts** tend to do well in action-oriented environments, particularly where there are people to influence, manage or control. Introverts tend to be less impulsive and more prepared to consider and reflect before acting.

■ The degree of **criticality** you bring to work will often indicate the kinds of tasks and organizational cultures that suit you best. If you are strongly driven by logic then systems and processes will often have high appeal. Those with low criticality tend to be more influenced by the feelings of others, and very much in tune with why relationships succeed or fail.

I All work requires a degree of **organization** – but some people are more comfortable with structure and timetables, while others like to keep life flexible and possibly even enjoy interruptions to the routine of life.

I Your **intellectual focus** reveals whether you are a grounded, pragmatic kind of person, or whether you like to think about underlying theories. Are you the sort of person that says 'if it ain't broke, don't fix it', or the kind who is keen to try out new ideas in the workplace?

I Your **emotional involvement** will often be a good indicator of how you cope with criticism in the workplace, and how you cope with rejection when your 'offer' isn't accepted. On the plus side, this with high scores in this area tend to be energized and passionate about the work they do.

F. Examine your attitudes and values

We all take our values to work with us. Your **values** are expressed in work through the tasks and outcomes you find interesting and meaningful. Sometimes this is on a macro scale – you're interested in what your company makes and how it contributes to the world. For others values are expressed in relationships at work and the way staff are treated. Ultimately, staff are more motivated in work situations where the organization and their colleagues share most of their values.

Our survey in **Chapter 2** also revealed the power of the right attitude at work. Think about what you feel, and what you show. If you are more introverted than others, you will tend not to display your feelings. Sometimes, if you're also a fairly theoretical person, you will sit and listen to ideas without communicating very much. These are elements that matter when it comes to attitude: what you show is more important than what you feel. If you have people around you who need to *hear* and *see* encouragement, make sure they do so.

In today's work environment, attitude is often focused on the way you feel about change. The important question is how do others *believe* that you feel about change? Business gurus often tell us that the most important driver in a business is the willingness of staff to commit to change. You don't have to be a deep-down enthusiast for a change-a-minute workplace, but resistance to change may well be a Career-Limiting Action (see **Chapter 10**).

Marketing recruiter Linda Clark says: 'Be reasonably conformist, which demonstrates that you fit in, while at the same time show that you add real value to the organization.'

'MUST DO' LIST

☑ Look at how far your career to date has been limited by your own dominant picture of what a 'career' is, and how it's supposed to work.

☑ Explore the options available to you if you think outside these rules.

☑ Work through your DIY career review. Getting others to help will add to your insights.

☑ Find out more about your personality. How well do you work in a team? (See also **Chapter 11**.)

☑ How well does your working style and preferences match your boss and colleagues?

☑ How could you make a significant difference to your job in the next 6 months?

What's Driving You?

This chapter helps you to:

▌ Look at success in your terms

▌ Find out what really motivates you

▌ Set and achieve real goals

▌ Understand your career drivers

▌ Begin to renegotiate elements of your job

Chance favours the prepared mind.

Louis Pasteur

I WANT TO BE SUCCESSFUL

As **Chapter 2** indicated, being successful in your career means different things to different people. In the broadest terms, it means receiving some kind of external validation of what you have achieved. In the past this was usually measured by money or status, but we live in a society where the relationship between people and work is complicated. We want more out of work, and different kinds of validation. Men and women often 'read' careers quite differently, expecting different outcomes. We seek rewards in different ways at different times of our lives.

Our idea of career success might be defined in a number of ways:

■ I want to be recognized for the skills I have to offer.

■ I want to be able to provide for my family.

■ I want to be happy at work.

■ I want to make a difference.

■ I want to be well paid.

■ I want to be in a senior position in an organization.

■ I want to run my own show.

■ I want to develop a national or international reputation.

■ I want to have control over my life.

■ I want to make things happen.

■ I want to work with people who share my values.

■ I want to win.

UNDERSTANDING WHAT MOTIVATES *YOU*

It's likely that your picture of what you want to get out of your career has changed at least a little during the course of your working life. With our first job we tend to focus on the surface aspects of work: receiving a pay cheque, having a job title, fitting into an organization. Later on we start to think about what work is really about.

Our career drivers are the psychological factors that prompt us to want to work, and the reasons we want to work.

In 1910 a London newspaper ran the following advertisement:

WANTED: volunteers for a hazardous journey. Small wages. Bitter cold. Long months of complete darkness. Safe return doubtful. Honour and recognition in case of success.

There were 10,000 applications for 20 positions on Shackleton's expedition to the South Pole. Who says that money and security are life's main motivators?

EXERCISE 4.1 – THE 3-MINUTE MOTIVATION CHECKLIST

What motivates you to get up in the morning and go to work? Look at **Table 4.1**. Imagine that you have £20 to spend on yourself, and you can spread that £20 on any or all of the things that really motivate you in work, taken from the list below. You can allocate £20 to one motivator, or spread it among as many as you like, but don't use units smaller than £1.

Table 4.1 3-Minute Motivation Checklist

Motivating factor	£££s
1 **Status** My worth is recognized in my job title/pay level/car/responsibilities …	
2 **Recognition** I am recognized for my skills and contribution	
3 **Feedback** I know when I am doing a good job	
4 **Skills balance** My opportunities and skills are well matched	
5 **Challenge** I like to take on new projects and problems	
6 **Success** I enjoy being a winner	
7 **Personal development** I have continuing opportunities to learn and stretch myself	
8 **Variety** My work is varied and interesting	

Continued

Table 4.1 (Contd)

Motivating factor	£££s
9 **Responsibility** I am responsible for important things/people/projects	
10 **Company values** I recognize and agree with the values of my employer	
11 **Independence/freedom** I have some control over how I spend my time at work and where I go	
12 **Fun** I am totally absorbed in what I do	
13 **Team membership** I enjoy being part of an active, supportive team	
14 **Making a difference/contributing** I can see what my contribution adds to the whole process	
15 **Helping others** My work contributes to others, or to society as a whole	
16 **Meaning and fulfilment** I find my work meaningful and fulfilling	
17 **Security** Knowing what I will be doing and earning in a year's time matters to me	
18 **Earnings now** I am relatively well paid in comparison with my peers	
19 **Earnings potential** My earnings will probably increase significantly in the future.	
20 **Fringe benefits** The job has interesting perks.	

> Look at where you have allocated your scores in **Table 4.1**. Imagine now that you are in a job and the money issues are resolved. You are being paid what you feel you deserve, and you have reasonable prospects of pay increases in the future. If you have allocated any score to the bottom three lines, boxes 18–20, now reallocate these £££s to any other motivators on the list.

Money and motivation

If a friend asks you what you want out of a career move, it's simple and easy to say 'more money'. Probe behind that answer and you usually get to the true motivators – the buttons an employer needs to press in order to get you to act more enthusiastically, to go the extra mile. These are also the factors that will ultimately persuade you to stay in a job or move on – the steps an organization needs to take to retain you.

Why do we consider and then sidestep the issue of money? It's because money for most people is a weak motivator. I regularly run workshops for sales staff, and ask them to imagine that it is mid-December and they have just been awarded a 10% pay increase with effect from 1 January. How long, I ask, will the pay rise motivate them to perform better? Usually the answer varies from 2 to 4 weeks. We all get a thrill when the extra pay comes through in our first pay slip, but after that a raise has very little impact on performance.

Even a shiny new company car has a limited impact for most workers. By the time you've shown the car to family and friends and it's been through the car wash, for most of us it's no longer prompting an improved performance.

Now turn the situation around. Imagine it's mid-December and your boss says: 'It's been a rough year, and sadly I am going to have to ask you to take a 10% pay cut from January'. How often would you remember? Every time you had a pay slip, and every time you saw a job advertised in the newspaper.

How long do you think that a pay cut has a *negative* effect on performance? Most workshop participants usually say 'until I get a new job'.

There is, however, a small proportion of workers who are capable of constantly remotivating themselves around financial targets. Often they do this by competing against themselves, constantly resetting the stopwatch and chasing new targets. If you have someone like that making money for you, it's a good idea to hang on to him or her!

Focusing on your motivators

Look again at the list of motivators in **Table 4.1**. What will really encourage you to give more at work? How do you like to receive external validation? Does your present role provide you with what you are looking for? (The 3-Minute Motivation Checklist only provides a rough sketch of your career drivers. For a more detailed breakdown see **Exercise 4.2** at the end of this chapter.)

Some factors are powerful if they are present, some are more powerful by their absence. For example, pleasant working conditions rarely motivate people to work harder, but moving someone into a dark, dingy environment will almost certainly have a negative impact on performance.

Why do we misunderstand motivation?

It's interesting to compare the way that employers and their staff perceive motivation. The issue of motivation has been studied from the perspective of both employees and managers. In one study, by Thomas Crane and Lerissa Patrick (*The Heart of Coaching: Using Transformational Coaching to Create a High-Performance Culture, 2002*) managers were asked to guess what motivated their workforce. Employees placed 'Appreciation' and 'Feeling "in" on things' as their top two factors. Managers predicted that money was the top motivator for their workforce, followed by job security. Do managers, once being promoted to supervisory positions, forget what it is like to be an employee? Almost inevitably managers feel they have to deal with money and promotion issues because that's what they spend most of their time talking about when they are negotiating around job roles. This is useful to know, because it is often far easier for your boss to improve the non-financial aspects of your job.

You can't expect a busy manager to read your motivators. Ultimately it's your task to communicate what motivates you, and to negotiate with your employer so you increase the number of motivators in your work, and decrease the things that turn you off.

How might your company say thank you?

Look at the ways past employers have tried to motivate you: by incentives, pay, or praise? Perhaps by other non-financial rewards including learning opportunities. How many of these have been successful? How long did the motivation last? On the other hand, look at those aspects of work which demotivate you: how long does that affect your work performance?

Work is a deal. You offer your time and energy and commitment and an employer provides you with a range of benefits and opportunities in return. The range of things an employer can offer is perhaps broader than you think. Some of the items on the following list will in fact cost your employer very little.

Rewards/opportunities you might try to negotiate

▌ Increased flexibility, e.g. flexitime, or finishing early one day a week.

▌ Learning opportunities (funding, supporting or encouraging courses you do, whether undertaken in working hours or not).

▌ Training opportunities.

▌ Specific kinds of work experience that enlarge your CV.

▌ Better feedback and support from your line manager.

▌ A mentor or coach to improve your work effectiveness.

▌ Work shadowing and job rotation to increase your work awareness and skill level.

▌ Attachment to teams and projects you find interesting.

▌ Opportunities to work alongside and learn from top performers.

▌ Opportunities to initiate and manage new projects.

▌ Opportunities to travel, or to work with and visit other
organizations.

▌ Additional holidays, paid or unpaid.

You can discover more about negotiating different aspects of
your job in **Chapter 9**. One of the ways of looking at this issue
is to think of your job as a series of commitment zones, as
shown in **Figure 4.1** and explained in **Table 4.2**.

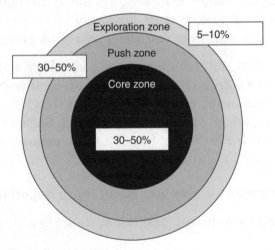

Figure 4.1 Commitment zones

Table 4.2 Commitment zones

Time	Your perspective	Employer perspective
30–50% core zone	Some of this may be routine, but it needs to be done, and failure to complete this work will give you difficulties with your boss.	Covers the basic elements of the role. The job gets done; you're a safe pair of hands.
30–50% push zone	Time where your employer may be pushing you outside the obvious remit of the job – asking you to go the extra mile, bring more enthusiasm and commitment.	Your willingness to respond, within reasonable limits, influences the picture your employer has of you.
5–10% exploration zone	Your personal playpen – opportunities to try out new roles and ideas and explore career possibilities.	You will usually have to persuade your employer to give you this freedom, and communicate the benefits before and after you do it.

Although your exploration zone is small, it can have huge leverage on the rest of your career. Spending just 5% of your time on role development means you can learn several new skills in a year, and attach yourself to at least one new project every few months.

Looking at commitment zones is helpful because it focuses on expectations – yours and your employer's. We look at this trade-off in much more detail in **Chapter 5**. Other chapters discuss ways you can use your 'exploration zone' to expand the boundaries of your job, and **Chapter 11** looks at ways of using this time to explore new career possibilities.

SETTING REAL GOALS

Goals and dreams

As soon as you begin to look at your commitment to the job, you see that you need to focus on activities that matter. Setting real goals is about sorting out the difference between fantasy and reality. We all have daydreams – sometimes they are an important distraction from routine and dull activities. You might dream of living in a beach hut in the West Indies, or running a second-hand bookshop in New York, or winning Formula 1. Daydreams are a necessary entertainment. But one of the things we like about them is the fact that we do not have do actually do anything about the daydream. It is a pure, self-enclosed fantasy.

Goals are rather different. There is no point having a goal unless you are prepared to explore ways of achieving it. Indeed, many would say that there is no point having goals unless you are prepared to *do* something about them.

A goal is something you can move towards. In fact, you can clearly see that there is a series of footsteps between you and a real goal. It's possible to imagine and plan the step just before you achieve your goal, and the step before that. Once you begin to visualize those footsteps you are forced to come to the conclusion that there is a step right in front of you. For most of us taking that step requires a conversation – finding something out, seeking out someone who has already achieved or discovered something, recruiting a mentor or coach. The powerful thing about the next step principle is that you have to discover a powerful reason not to take it – and it's much harder to resist one step than several.

EIGHT STEPS TO GOAL SETTING

Begin with blue-sky thinking. What would you really like to do? Where would you like to get within your organization? It's widely recognized that the first, critical step is to define your goals and write them down. **Table 4.3** shows you the steps involved, set out in reverse order from the point of goal achievement and working backwards to the first action.

Table 4.3 From goal back to first steps

8 **Begin with the end in mind.** Imagine what it feels just after you have achieved your goal. If your ambition is to give a public performance, imagine the moment after you have finished and been successful. Experience the feelings that will come immediately after you have achieved your goal.

7 **Look at the outcome.** How outlandish/unrealistic/outside your comfort zone is this goal? How will you feel if you are retired and you haven't got there – or never tried?

6 **Look at the last steps.** Imagine the final steps you have to take. The last moments before reaching the top of the mountain. The moment you are called on stage to accept your award. The day you put your key in the door of your own business.

5 **Look at the intermediate steps.** What will you have to do on the way? What will you need to learn? Looking at this stage allows you to deal with the practical things you need to do to get from A to Z.

4 **Look at the barriers.** Imagine looking back at life from a time when you have achieved your goal. Look at the time between now and your goal as if it was history. What were the greatest obstacles? What did you have to do to overcome them? What kind of knockbacks did you get? Who tried to put you off your goals? How did you deal with rejection and criticism?

3 **What are the first steps?** If your goal is going to become reality, what do you need to do in the next 6 months? Remember to give yourself incentives for each step, and recruit people to do some encouraging.

2 **What is your immediate priority?** What do you need to do right away? Who do you need to speak to? Where do you put your first footstep?

1 **Why do you want to change?** Look at where you are now and **Step 8**, where you want to be. What happens if you do nothing?

EXERCISE 4.2 – YOUR CAREER DRIVERS

What do you really want to get out of work? Complete Table 4.4 to work out your detailed career drivers.

Table 4.4 Your career drivers

CODE		Write your score in this column: 3 for Essential 2 for Very Important 1 for Of Some Importance 0 for Not Important or Irrelevant
S	STABILITY Staying in one job a while	
S	SECURITY Being able to plan financially	
S	LARGE ORGANIZATION A 'steady' employer	
S	STATED GOALS Clear targets and objectives	

Table 4.4 (Contd)

CODE	Write your score in this column: 3 for **Essential** 2 for **Very Important** 1 for **Of Some Importance** 0 for **Not Important or Irrelevant**
S ROUTINE Predictable daily workload	TOTAL **S** SCORE:

Table 4.4 (Contd)

CODE		Write your score in this column: 3 for **Essential** 2 for **Very Important** 1 for **Of Some Importance** 0 for **Not Important or Irrelevant**
A	WORKING ALONE In my own time and space	
A	DIRECTING MY OWN WORK Not being micro-managed	
A	POWER TO DECIDE Authority to make key decisions	
A	TIME FREEDOM Controlling my diary, setting my own deadlines	
A	INDEPENDENCE Doing things my way in my time	
		TOTAL **A** SCORE:

Table 4.4 (Contd)

CODE		Write your score in this column: **3 for Essential** **2 for Very Important** **1 for Of Some Importance** **0 for Not Important or Irrelevant**
P	**HELPING SOCIETY** As a whole, or one particular community	
P	**BUILDING COMMUNITY** Putting something back in	
P	**SERVING OTHERS** Putting my skills at the service of those with the greatest need	
P	**MAKING A DIFFERENCE** Making a personal contribution to an issue or problem	
P	**HELPING THE ENVIRONMENT** A job that is environmentally conscious or friendly	
		TOTAL P SCORE:

Table 4.4 (Contd)

CODE		Write your score in this column: 3 for Essential 2 for Very Important 1 for Of Some Importance 0 for Not Important or Irrelevant
E	BUILDING SOMETHING FROM SCRATCH Creating something new	
E	MAKING MONEY For myself and others	
E	LAUNCHING NEW IDEAS New products or services	
E	RUNNING MY OWN SHOW My own unit or my own business	
E	EXCITEMENT The buzz of activity or challenge	
		TOTAL E SCORE:

Table 4.4 (Contd)

CODE		Write your score in this column: 3 for **Essential** 2 for **Very Important** 1 for **Of Some Importance** 0 for **Not Important or Irrelevant**
M	INFLUENCING PROGRESS Taking things in the right direction	
M	MASTERING CHANGE Coping with rapid change	
M	RAPID PACE Enjoying life in the fast lane	
M	TARGETS Need a new challenge every day	
M	CONTINUOUS IMPROVEMENT Believing there's always a better way	
		TOTAL **M** SCORE:

Table 4.4 (Contd)

CODE	Write your score in this column: 3 for Essential 2 for Very Important 1 for Of Some Importance 0 for Not Important or Irrelevant
C	CHAMPIONING INNOVATION Promoting new thinking	
C	THINKING OUTSIDE THE BOX Using lateral thinking	
C	INVENTION Coming up with new concepts	
C	BEING ARTISTIC Doing this artistically, with a sense of balance and design	
C	NEW ANGLE Seeing things afresh, having a new take on things	
		TOTAL **C** SCORE:

Table 4.4 (Contd)

CODE		Write your score in this column: 3 for Essential 2 for Very Important 1 for Of Some Importance 0 for Not Important or Irrelevant
L	FAMILY Work that is good for family life	
L	TIME BALANCE Leaving time and energy after work	
L	COMMUTING & TRAVEL Limiting the time I spend travelling to or for work	
L	WELL-BEING Time and space to be healthier	
L	LOCATION Working the right distance from home	
		TOTAL **L** SCORE:

Table 4.4 (Contd)

CODE		Write your score in this column: **3 for Essential** **2 for Very Important** **1 for Of Some Importance** **0 for Not Important or Irrelevant**
D	INFLUENCING PEOPLE Changing hearts and minds	
D	INFLUENCING DECISIONS Being 'in the loop'	
D	DRIVING PEOPLE & SYSTEMS Getting the best out of people and systems	
D	LEADING PEOPLE Leading from the front	
D	COMPETITION Keeping a competitive edge	
		TOTAL **D** SCORE:

Table 4.4 (Contd)

CODE		Write your score in this column: **3 for Essential** **2 for Very Important** **1 for Of Some Importance** **0 for Not Important or Irrelevant**
X	BEING AN EXPERT in my specialism	
X	BEING CONSULTED For my expertise	
X	SPECIALIST KNOWLEDGE Being an information broker or specialist	
X	PROBLEM SOLVING Trouble-shooting, relying on my knowledge	
X	SETTING STANDARDS In my industry or specialism	
		TOTAL **X** SCORE:

Table 4.4 (Contd)

CODE	Write your score in this column: **3 for Essential** **2 for Very Important** **1 for Of Some Importance** **0 for Not Important or Irrelevant**
R	**RECOGNITION** Being noticed for what I do
R	**SALARY INCREMENTS** A clear ladder to better pay
R	**STANDARD OF LIVING** Others can see I am doing well
R	**HIGH FINANCIAL REWARDS** Earning as much as I can
R	**REPUTATION** Being highly regarded by others
	TOTAL **R** SCORE:

Table 4.4 (Contd)

CODE		Write your score in this column: 3 for Essential 2 for Very Important 1 for Of Some Importance 0 for Not Important or Irrelevant
I	**RELATIONSHIPS** Building up good relationships at work	
I	**TEAM WORK** Being a player in a great team	
I	**ENCOURAGING** Getting the best out of others	
I	**BUILDING PEOPLE** A 'learning organization', a development culture	
I	**CARING FOR PEOPLE** Believing that people matter	
		TOTAL I SCORE:

How to interpret your results

Add up the scores you have for each code and include them in **Table 4.5** to establish your main driver types. Then identify your top five in an approximate rank order. Don't worry if you have equal scores: everyone is a mix of different kinds of motivation.

Table 4.5 Career driver types

Code	Driver type	Score	Rank order
S	Stability and security		
A	Autonomy – doing things on your own, or your way		
P	Purpose and meaning		
E	Enterprise and action		
M	Change Master – driving change, and thriving on it		
C	Creativity		
L	Life/work balance		
D	Drive/influence		
X	Expertise/specialisms		
R	Reward and recognition		
I	Interaction with people		

EXERCISE 4.2 – Setting goals focused on your career drivers

1. Refer back to **Table 4.4**.

2. Examine the items you gave a score of zero. Is there anything you actively want to avoid?

3. Look at of the items you gave a score of 3. Decide on in your top 10, and list them in **Table 4.6** as your top 10 career drivers.

4. In column 2 of **Table 4.6**, indicate how far each driver is met in your present role. How could you do your job differently to increase the scores in column 2? What goals can you now set yourself to begin the process of changing your job?

5. How closely does this top 10 relate to your choices in the 3-Minute Motivator (**Exercise 4.1**)?

Table 4.6 Your Top 10 Career Drivers

My top 10 career drivers	How far is this driver met by your present job? ✓✓ = fully ✓ = moderately ✗ = not at all

'MUST DO' LIST: BUILDING ON YOUR MOTIVATORS

☑ What really motivates you? At work? Outside work? Work out the factors that really do encourage long-term commitment. As far as work is concerned, what motivates you to get out of bed on a winter morning?

☑ If you were your boss, what would you have to do to retain you? Think about the ways you would like your job to grow and change.

☑ What is the best way for your employer to reward you? Once the money issues are resolved (and especially if they are not) how do you like to be thanked? Think of what you would really find encouraging and helpful.

☑ Which commitment zones do you work in most of the time? Are you experimenting with at least a small proportion of your time as a 'Push Zone'?

Solving Employers' Problems

This chapter helps you to:

▌ Review how well you know your organization

▌ Begin to see work from an employer's perspective

▌ See how you can maximize your impact at work

▌ Focus on outcomes as well as objectives

▌ Manage your time to achieve the right results

There is nothing so useless as doing efficiently that which should not be done at all.

Peter Drucker

THE BIG PICTURE

Too many careers founder because workers don't have a big enough picture of the work they do. They focus on the job as a job, or as part of a department or team. It's too easy to look just at the micro level of the job description. Even when we broaden the view to take in departmental goals, you may still not be making a contribution that has the biggest leverage: in other words, not just *doing things right* but *doing the right things*. Your job needs to contribute to the organization as a whole – and people need to notice.

In the previous chapter we looked at the factors that make you work with more energy. This chapter helps you to direct that energy so that it is focused on the needs of your employer. As a result you will learn to focus on key result areas, to work effectively with more focus on the organization, using time management techniques to create more 'wins'.

Coaching specialist Stuart Carter reflects on the three steps that had presented him as being more in tune with organizational objectives: '(1) Ensure that personal achievements contribute strongly to the company strategy and targets. (2) Learn, digest and focus on the key items you need to deliver on – if you have targets understand clearly what actions you need to take that will have the maximum influence on those targets. (3) Don't be afraid of blowing your own trumpet.'

Consultant engineer Nigel Lloyd recommends that you make sure that you deliver: 'ensure that you actually do what you say you will do. Make it clear to all your work contacts that you are committed to the tasks you undertake. Being able to achieve this necessarily means that you need to think carefully before agreeing to deliverables – it is amazing how many people do not adequately evaluate before committing to a course of action.'

Key Result Areas

Your job description may say a lot about duties and responsibilities, but only limited information about Key Result Areas (KRAs). Sometimes known as Key Performance Indicators, these are an organization's way of measuring individual, unit and total performance.

Carole Pemberton, author and Founder of Career Matters, suggests that you find a 'third person position' and look at yourself objectively – 'how strong is your currency within your work? Are you offering what the organization now wants?'

Whether you are negotiating a new role or discussing a job you've done for some time, the questions in **Table 5.1** will be helpful both to you and to your manager.

Table 5.1   Questions around Key Result Areas

---

1 What is the purpose of the job?
Why is this job here at all? What headache, problem or opportunity does it address?

2 What does the job contribute?
What leverage does this job exert?

3 How does the job fit into the organization?
How does my work depend on/impact upon others?

4 What specific skills or knowledge are required?
What else do I need to learn to be successful? Who is available who already has these skills or knowledge?

5 What are the main problems to be solved?
What can go wrong? What skills will I need to fix problems? How did previous post holders survive?

6 How much freedom is there to act or make decisions?
How much space do I have to use my initiative?

7 What controls or limits apply to the job?
What are budgetary, organizational or time constraints?

8 What quick wins are expected and possible?
What results need to be achieved quickly – and how will they be measured?

8 What results does the job exist to achieve? How is performance measured?
What are the long-term outcomes – how will they be measured? Who will judge what is meant by success?

9 Who needs to be influenced to achieve a result?
Who will support the outcome, and who will get in the way?

10 How should the result be communicated?
Who does the outcome need to be communicated to? How?

As **Table 5.1** makes clear, there are many questions to be asked to ensure success. Don't make the mistake of thinking it's just about hard work.

Mike Eastwood, Liverpool Diocesan Secretary, adds: 'I have long taken the view that the best (and often the hardest) people to recruit are those that will take responsibility for what they do. Therefore the best approaches to achieving career success centre on establishing a reputation early on for accepting responsibility and delivering.'

Understanding how your employer thinks is a vital part of the process, because then you can begin a dialogue between your personal goals and the organization's key result areas: in short, gaining career satisfaction while your employer achieves the right outcomes. Penny Chester, ACPI World President and Managing Consultant for Right Coutts, believes that what matters is 'commitment in the face of difficult or demanding circumstances, running the extra mile, integrity when organizational politics beckon, sound knowledge base and generosity in sharing it' – in other words, a focused application of individual skills and values to a particular work context.

Key Result Areas in different kinds of organization

If you work in a profit-oriented environment it's usually clear how your job is benchmarked: turnover, profitability, time or money saved. Some KRA's are more qualitative: customer satisfaction, for example, or retention rates. You may be given targets based on the way you manage and retain staff, or the ways you develop new business leads.

Many job descriptions avoid concrete benchmarks, preferring to use vague terms like 'contribute to …' and 'assist with …'. Some employers, particularly those in the public and not-for-profit sectors, include a mix of 'soft' (largely qualitative, and often subjective) and 'hard' (clear, measurable and unambiguous) outcomes. The first group is more difficult to handle. If you are supposed to 'liaise with' or 'ensure effective communication to' other staff, how do you know when you have been partially or completely successful? The difficulty here is that organizations feel under pressure to include KRAs in a job description, but then write them in such a way that no-one is very clear how anything will be measured.

The first step is to probe the goals and targets you've been given. What do they actually mean? How do others interpret them? What would your employer recognize as a result that was acceptable, or even exceptional? To win at this game inevitably means delving deep into the organizational culture to find out what the words used in your KRAs actually mean.

Reading your organization in a different way

A short cut to identifying KRAs is to look at your organization in a new light. Research your employer as if it were a major new account you were trying to win. If you wanted to win a big piece of business from a company, your research would be thorough: key people at the top and their backgrounds, the organization's main themes and targets, and a list of recent achievements and future projects. How many of us really undertake that kind of basic research with our own organization? We adopt a passive approach: 'I'll be told everything I need to know', rather than hunting down data that can show us with great clarity where to make our contribution.

Executive recruiter Andrew Tallents, Director of Warren Partners, goes even further: 'I have done due diligence on every company I have considered joining. This includes finding out as much about the culture and the future for the business as possible. I have not looked at just the base salary of the role but the opportunity for progression. I have looked at the people I will be working with and identified what I would need to do to progress and hence achieve career development.'

Getting the right kind of results means *working hard on doing the things that matter*.

How aware are you of your employer's needs?

Table 5.2 offers you a chance to work out how in tune you are with the key facts about your present employer.

Table 5.2 How Much Do you Know About Your Employer?

Key questions	Very aware	Moder- ately aware	I need to discover things fairly quickly
Who are the top decision-makers in your organization?			
Who is likely to retire within the next 2 years?			
Who is likely to be promoted to a key position within the next 2 years?			
What competencies are listed by your employer in connection with top performers?			
How did your employer begin? – What are its origins?			
What is your employer's Mission Statement?			
What is your employer's best/worst selling product or service?			

Table 5.2 (Contd)

Key questions	Very aware	Moderately aware	I need to discover things fairly quickly
How profitable is your employer compared to others in its market sector?			
How has the share price of your company performed compared to its closest competitors?			
What is your employer's most/least profitable activity?			
What is your employer's biggest customer?			
Who is your employer's biggest competitor?			
What is your organization's market share?			
What are your employer's strongest brand values?			
What differentiates your employer from your closest competitors?			
What trade or professional associations have strong links with your employer?			
What major new products or services are likely to come on line in the next 12 months?			

Table 5.2   (Contd)

Key questions	Very aware	Moder-ately aware	I need to discover things fairly quickly
What new products or services from competitors are likely to impact on your employer?			
What new legislation is coming along which may affect your employer or your job?			
What is your employer's track record for staff retention, recruitment, and training?			
Who makes most of the decisions about staff development and training in your organization?			
Who else in your organization performs a similar role to you in a different department or division?			
What reputation does the press have of your employer's products, services, and values??			
Who are the key people who know the answers to most of the above questions – people you need to speak to within the next month?			

OBJECTIVES AND OUTCOMES

Focus on objectives

Most management courses tell you that to succeed you need to set objectives. It's important to say what you mean by success, and knowing when you have got there. Your job may have explicit objectives. These might be expressed on a functional level (to check and process 100 application forms) or may be linked to quality standards (achieving above-average customer satisfaction ratings). The best kinds of objectives are *measurable* (so you know when you've hit them), and are *planned* – you know what you have to do to reach them. Better still, objectives should be related to the bigger picture – where your organization is going.

José Arnó, a Spanish career coach and author, suggests that you should be 'proactive but also prudent. Think like an entrepreneur not like an employee – identify ways and make proposals to improve efficiency, fearlessly taking on the tasks that your proposals involve.'

Workers who see the way they contribute to the bottom line usually work more effectively. The very best kinds of objectives are also linked to motivation. We all know about setting SMART objectives (Specific, Measurable, Achievable, Realistic, and Timebound) – the basics of good objective setting. But do you really feel like getting out of bed on a cold winter's morning to fulfil objectives that are simply specific, measurable, achievable … ? Possibly not. We also need objectives that are *energizing* and *rewarding*. SmartER objectives make work more interesting.

Outcomes sometimes beat objectives

You're already aware that career awareness is about changing things in a short timescale, and looking at quick wins. First, let's agree one principle: businesses are built around perceptions, not facts.

Most surveys about customer relationships tell you that the main reason a customer leaves you isn't quality, price, or promptness. In surveys the majority of customers say they switched to another supplier largely because they *felt* they weren't being looked after.

Think about buying a meal in a restaurant. An objective-driven approach to getting your meal in front of you will focus on measurable standards: food temperature, quality, visual presentation, time from order to service, etc. However, what really matters is that we walk out of the restaurant feeling we had a good experience. That's less about conformity to standards, and more about feeling that we were made to feel welcome and slightly special by the restaurant staff. In that atmosphere all food tastes better. Customer loyalty to brands and services is more about feelings than facts.

This has important implications for your career, especially if you have always believed that success is about measurable objectives. These will be noted, but won't set the world on fire. Objective setting is an important building block in business, but the most successful businesses (and the most successful workers) also have an instinctive understanding outcomes. People tick objectives but remember outcomes.

A departmental meeting will have objectives (getting through the agenda, commissioning new projects, allocating workloads, seeking ideas or information and so on), however a meeting will also have important outcomes, for example whether people get on better with each other, and whether people are more informed, more motivated, more committed than they were at the outset. With some teams being able to work together is just as important as what you are working on. What if you can create a better outcome by breaking the rules, or by not holding the meeting at all?

This works for relationships with your boss, too. If your boss wants to looks good or feel reassured, then work towards that outcome. If your boss has a particular hobby-horse (wants you to be in work before her in the morning, hates surprises, wants you to remember people's names, or likes you to have a perfectly tidy desk), achieving that outcome may be more powerful than anything else in your job description. Work with the grain rather than against it. Sometimes the key to success is being able to think like your boss (or your boss's boss) thinks. This isn't simply about buzzwords, but about realizing what your boss finds important, focusing on your boss's biggest headache, and solving the problem. The main thing is that your boss sees that you are playing by the same rules and with the same objectives in mind.

ALIGNING YOURSELF WITH THE ORGANIZATION

Learn the local language

For Bill Walmsley, Business Development Director of CERTT, success was about 'recognizing that organizations (invariably) behave according to an often unwritten cultural code – presenting business cases in a manner consistent with the code is essential in gaining support for career enhancing initiatives.'

Managers often criticize their subordinates saying that X 'isn't on board' or Y 'doesn't get it' – the employer and individual seem to be speaking different languages. Start to become aware of the language that key people in your organization use. What is the dominant set of metaphors? Whether your company is into 'road maps' or 'cutting-edge thinking' or 'empowerment', it often helps to begin to match your language with the kind of language used by key players. Done with some subtlety and understanding, this goes a long way to communicating the fact that you are sensitive to your employer's KRAs.

Becoming more in tune with your organization is like learning the nuances of a very local dialect. Look at the language that is used by your organization. Are you in tune with this year's buzzwords? Your ability to use these terms in an intelligent way indicates your success in really thinking about the major concerns, problems and opportunities of your organization.

'Lots of companies are going through structural change at the moment', says executive recruiter Linda Clark, 'try to find out where the organization is focused and set yourself up to be in the team which is going to be the centre of the strategy. Join up for something nobody else wants to do.'

Use the 10% principle

The 10% principle works like this. If you want to set up a new sandwich shop in your local area, you don't hunt around for a high street where there are no other sandwich shops. You find one where there is a busy sandwich shop. There is already a clientele, already a flow of business, and nobody needs persuading that buying a freshly made sandwich is a good idea. To compete you need to do use the 10% principle. To succeed you only need to be 10% *something*: 10% cheaper, 10% better quality, 10% faster, or have 10% more choice of sandwich fillings.

How can you use this principle in your job? Think of your employer as your customer, and others around you as suppliers. What can you do 10% better, faster, or more creatively? In an organization this approach will work far better if used in co-operation rather than competitively – if someone is doing something successfully, ask if you can join in and bring your ideas to the party. If you are comparing your offer with an external supplier, you have a very strong offer on your hands: something that can be done better by bringing it in house.

Early warning system

Look at some of the problems around you at work at the moment. How much easier would they have been to fix when they were minor problems? Perhaps you have a problem with a supplier who is under-performing and delivering late. What were the early warning signs that there was going to be a problem? Hindsight has 20/20 vision, as we know – so surely it's better to put in place some kind of early warning system?

Executive recruiter and careers author John Courtis' advice is: 'Doing things right and on time or telling peers and boss *in advance* if it cannot be done thus. Making constructive suggestions promptly rather than whingeing later is good too. Be a "can-do" person when it's possible and be sure to tell people crisply if they're asking the impossible or the unnecessary. You'll build respect from the people who matter.'

The early warning principle would wreck most disaster movies. Someone would notice the smouldering wires in the skyscraper, or the airline pilot's early symptoms of food poisoning. When warned not to approach Dracula's castle, the young couple in the forest would turn around and find a B&B. If you can spot the small signals that indicate trouble ahead, you've discovered a quick win, and something that gets you noticed. Don't do it too often, though, and be seen as a prophet of doom.

Peter Bell suggests: 'Always ensuring your superiors are never surprised by events or results helps to ensure their confidence in their position and in you. There are some setbacks that are unavoidable; if superiors are prepared they are seen to be on top of things and therefore confident in your abilities.'

BEING CLEAR ABOUT THE STARTING POINT

SWOT your situation

SWOT analysis is a handy tool for spotting employer's problems and KRAs. Use it to look at your own department, unit or team. Begin with the everyday information that is readily available to you and your colleagues – the way you work, your

Figure 5.1   SWOT analysis

biggest customers, your biggest headaches. Take the initiative and suggest using a SWOT at your next team meeting.

A SWOT analysis (see **Figure 5.1**) begins by looking at the current strengths and weaknesses of an organization or team. Question 1: what happens if nothing changes? At this stage you are focused on internal factors, and remember to look at all of the strengths of your situation: your colleagues, your resources, your client base. **Strengths** will probably include key staff, retained knowledge and expertise, and may include other factors like brand strengths and market position. **Weaknesses** often arise because it's difficult to hang on to any of these strengths; people leave, and know-how becomes stale or out of date. Weaknesses also arise from gaps in service or under-staffing. It may also be about weak administration or bureaucratic obstacles. You may be the first one at your level in the organization to wake up and smell the coffee.

The lower half of the SWOT diagram looks at *external factors*, and also looks at *future* possibilities. What opportunities have already presented themselves that you have yet to exploit? What threats can you perceive?

This exercise works well on a small-scale level because you are often able to do something with the results. You may be concerned about what you do when you discover negatives – what do you do with this information? Remember that you will contribute directly to KRAs by spotting **early warning signals** (see above). SWOT analysis is also great at generating **quick wins** (see **Chapter 12** for more details).

Using **SWOT** to highlight critical areas

A company can be very smug about **strengths**, so the most revealing (and disturbing) question sequence is 'What is your greatest, unique strength? And what is the *weakness inside that strength?*' For example, a company's greatest strength may be the features of its top-selling product. How quickly and easily can those features be imitated by competitors? How long can you maintain your position in the marketplace?

The analogy with your own career position is that you may take your strengths too much for granted. If you have a great relationship with a key manager, what happens if that manager moves on? If your strength is your technical ability, what happens if a consultant offers your company an even higher skill level? If your strength is your knowledge, how up to date is it? **Figure 5.2** shows you an example SWOT analysis applied to an individual.

GETTING TIME ON YOUR SIDE

In order to manage your workload, you need to manage your time, even if it's just about creating the time to research and deliver quick wins.

You've probably been on training programmes that promise to improve your performance through time management. Very few of them have really had an impact on performance in real

STRENGTHS	WEAKNESSES
• My client list • My sales skills • My contacts within the company **WEAKNESS INSIDE THE NO. 1 STRENGTH** • My clients could easily be reallocated to another consultant	• Lack of time to attend industry conferences • Long hours on the road mean I don't spend time with key managers in my company • My Divisional Manager doesn't know me very well **ACTION:** Schedule meeting with Divisional Manager to share my successes
OPPORTUNITIES	THREATS
• Spinning out new business from existing clients • Looking after my clients and checking service levels more personally to reduce the weakness inside my main strength **ACTION:** Focus on building client relationships	• External competitors • Rising stars in my own company • Divisional Manager wants to make cost (staff?) cuts **ACTION:** Learn from the most successful pitches and products of competitors

Figure 5.2 A SWOT approach to an individual career

terms. The principle that has maximum results is the 80/20 model, otherwise known as the Pareto principle. This principle applies to work and society; in most countries, for example, 80% of wealth and resources are owned by about 20% of the population. In work, 20% of your time produces about 80% of your results, as **Figure 5.3** reminds us. The flip side of this is that 80% of our time is relatively unproductive, gaining us only 20% of our results.

When you're thinking about contributing to your employer's KRAs, this approach really matters. Only 20% of your efforts at work will actually be effective in building up your reputation. Working out what exactly that effort constitutes, and how to

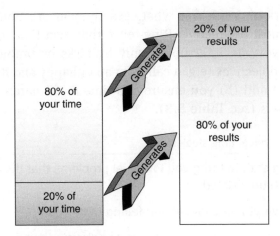

Figure 5.3   The 80/20 Principle

protect that vital time, is vital. Losing half of your 20% 'win time' can mean losing 40% of your contribution to success. Your visible, effective and most noticed productivity is achieved in just one-fifth of your working time. The problem is that if you lose any of this 'win time' to distractions, your results tail off dramatically.

How do you find your 'win time'? Look backwards, from the results. Look at the most important objectives you achieve, and the most significant outcomes. What did you do in order to achieve them? What exactly do you do in that time? And what gets in the way? Let's say that 8 hours a week achieve the greatest impact. If you allow this productive time to be cut in half, that has a huge leverage on your final results. The first and critical step in time management is to work out exactly what you are doing in your 20% 'win time', and protect that time as far as you can. If possible, extend it slightly. Persuade your boss to delegate to your strengths, not your weaknesses, and you will probably operate more securely in the 20% zone. Look at all of the things you do which are almost entirely unproductive. Cutting these activities back by as little as 30 minutes a week can create a huge impact on your end results.

The solution? Work out what, exactly, you are doing when you are most productive. Ring-fence that 'win time' to ensure (a) that you are interrupted only by tasks or problems that meet *key* objectives (e.g. a call from an unhappy and important customer) and (b) you ensure this time is not eaten away by *time stealers* (see **Table 5.3**).

Table 5.3   Typical time stealers

■ Allowing staff to bring you low level problems that they can deal with unassisted

■ Doing everything yourself and failing to delegate

■ Colleagues or subordinates trying to delegate to you

■ Overlapping responsibilities

■ Reinventing the wheel

■ Working to contradictory or fuzzy expectations

■ Allowing preferred tasks to distract from key activities

■ Failing to plan, so that everything is unexpected

■ Attending or calling unnecessary meetings

■ Junk mail (paper and electronic)

■ Failure to set a procedure for handling routine matters

■ Fatigue

■ Fighting fires, and never taking the time to focus on the small things that make the biggest difference

'MUST DO' LIST

☑ Work out the Key Result Areas in your job, your team, and your company.

☑ Where have you become too focused on objectives and missed the real outcomes?

☑ Agree your personal objectives with your line manager, then reflect on the outcomes that will be equally powerful.

☑ What early warning signals can you spot now that may prevent or limit problems ahead?

☑ What quick wins can you identify and deliver within the next 6 weeks?

☑ What activities really contribute to your 'win time'?

☑ Hunt down your main time stealers, and protect your 'win time'.

Being Visible

This chapter helps you to:

▌ Work out how others see you

▌ Improve your visibility

▌ Market yourself to your employer

▌ Communicate reasons why your employer should keep you on

▌ Manage occasions which move you on and up

Competition brings out the best in products and the worst in people.

David Sarnoff

IT'S ALL ABOUT COMMUNICATION

How disposable an asset are you?

As we saw in **Chapter 5**, being seen as a person with career prospects isn't about what you do, it's about employers noticing what you do. Skills alone are not enough.

Think of yourself as a corporate asset. A building, a piece of equipment, a vehicle. Disturbing isn't it? Suddenly you feel much more disposable. Companies boast that their people are their greatest asset. At times it seems that people are their greatest *disposable* asset. Why do we dispose of things? Because we feel we no longer have a use for them. We get rid of equipment, vehicles, buildings, even information when:

1. We haven't used them for a while.

2. They don't contribute directly to success.

3. They're a headache.

4. We can't remember why we got them in the first place.

Organizations make staff redundant for a huge variety of reasons. Sometimes there is some kind of restructuring, often the result of a merger or a change in the marketplace. At other times organizations shrink or change their focus. If that's the reality, there's little you can do about it except learn how to move on positively.

However, it's also true that companies use external reasons (like the marketplace, takeovers, new systems and so on) as an excuse to get rid of people who don't fit. Naturally, this is something they are unwilling to admit. On paper there are logical, publicly acceptably reasons for getting rid of particular people or departments, but it still seems to be the case that those people companies tend to get rid of first fit pretty well into one of the four categories above.

It's also true that the root cause behind a number of redundancy situations is problems between people. HR departments will find credible ways of wrapping it up, but at the heart of problems you can often find relationship difficulties, management problems, or people who have been set up to fail (see **Chapter 10**).

What can you do about it? It's important to begin by realizing that the need to communicate your strengths within an organization isn't just about achieving advancement. Sometimes it's about keeping your job. And it's always about being seen to be about making a direct and visible contribution – being seen as an asset.

In our survey, Business Link executive Helen Rodway gave the advice: 'be seen but don't be too opinionated, argumentative or verbose'.

I don't feel comfortable pushing myself forward

It's perfectly reasonable to have some hesitation about self-promotion. You begin by looking at the real purpose of the activity. Is it about you, or about the organization?

Look at the way top career performers market themselves rather than simply indulging in self-promotion. Self-promotion that is merely about *me*, about projecting my ego. We're really telling the world how important we are. Sometimes saying *I'm the best thing since sliced bread* gets your audience's attention, but it's important not to believe all your own PR.

Marketing as a discipline presents some useful parallels. True marketing isn't obsessed with the qualities and features of the product, but focuses on the needs of the buyer. it focuses on a question ('what do you need?') rather than a statement ('this is what we are selling'). Empty self-promotion is like unfocused selling – a hard sell that pushes something you don't really need or want. Empty self-promoters are like those telesales people who ring to sell you double glazing at the moment you sit down to supper. They have very little idea of what you need, or what will interest you; they just want to get through their sales script. Self-promoters spend more time talking than listening. They enjoy the sound of their own voices, and they enjoy the limelight. If they are interested in people's reactions, it's because they are interested in seeing a reflection of their own glory. The world is full of people who want to sell, but very few true marketeers.

Listening to others is a critical step. Jane Moorhouse, previously a senior executive with the NAAFI organization, suggests: 'Only share known facts with your team and don't gossip. Walk the floor and know everyone and their roles, don't force team building; listen.'

Table 6.1 Self-promotion vs marketing behaviours

Self-promotion behaviours	Marketing behaviours
I tell	I listen, then suggest
I am focused on, or even obsessed, with me	I am interested in my influence on the organization
I compete	I co-operate
I seek opportunities to win at the expense of others	I seek opportunities to find win/win with the organization
I promise the earth, then underperform or disappear	I underpromise, and overdeliver
I exploit weaknesses	I build on strengths
I speak this week's buzzwords	I am in tune with my organization's anxieties and ambitions
I put a spin on the facts	I present facts credibly and carry conviction
I convince people in the short term	I give people long-term evidence of my reliability
I move on and up	I make a lasting contribution and maintain relationships with former colleagues, bosses, and teams
I exploit other people	I enable others to work more effectively

Self-marketing: a more positive approach

You may hate self-promoters, and have a real reluctance to blow your own trumpet. But it's important to distinguish between self-promotion, which is ego driven, and the need we all have to become and remain visible to our employer.

This is a concept which is unfamiliar to most of us. Most behaviour seems to be polarized: some go for the 'keep your head down and work hard' approach, some push themselves forward rather too much. A small group of successful people instinctively learn a better approach – to *market yourself* to your own organization.

True marketing focuses on the needs of the customer, and that's what successful workers do. They begin by identifying and understanding their employers' biggest problems and greatest opportunities, and then communicate a match between what they have to offer and what the organization needs.

Self-marketers spend more time listening than talking. They discover. They listen to what people need. They pick up the right language, and become sensitive to the concerns and hopes of the organization. Most of all, they have a sense of perspective – the big picture. Whether your gift is managing the details or kick-starting the next project, always try to have a sense of how this contributes to your business in the widest sense – and if you don't know, find out.

Doesn't aggressive self-promotion sometimes work?

Sometimes the worst kind of self-promotion works, even when it's driven by vanity, narcissism and a Machiavellian lust for power. It's also true that the worst kind of sales techniques (pushy, insensitive, manipulative) do in fact work, as do the worst kind of management techniques (coercion, bullying, overbearing). It's equally true that fraud, deception and mugging old ladies can create an income stream. These methods get results, but often not in the long term, and always at a cost: to the person behaving this way, and to those on the receiving end.

So a word of warning: be aware that others will be competing around you who are true self-promoters. They will use every trick: ego massaging, manipulation, half-truths and lies. It's all too easy to acquiesce to this kind of behaviour, or – worse still – believe that this is the only behaviour that will get you success in your organization.

These issues are particularly important if you're trying to move up the ladder. I've heard a number of clients say *I don't want to be promoted – I've seen what you have to become.* They first need to question whether their colleagues really became something different, or whether they simply changed their behaviours. Sometimes you have to challenge the idea that there is only one kind of person who will succeed in your organization. Look at the full range of senior figures in business life, and you'll find that there are a wide range of personality types, and a wide range of personal values. You can find ethical and sensitive people at the highest levels (just as you can find mean-minded, bitter and self-obsessed people at every level in an organization). Three things, however, come out in most surveys of business leaders: they have the ability to deal with people, the ability to have a strong vision and work towards it, and they have sufficient personal strength to remain true to themselves throughout the ups and downs of the process.

If you are genuinely worried that the price to be paid for career advancement is unacceptable, you probably need to explore this further. Is it a genuine fear that you have negative characteristics which will be emphasized or exploited? If you have a tendency to cut corners or bend the truth, will you become really lazy or dishonest? Or is there something about the way you *read* the organization that makes you believe you will have to behave in unacceptable ways?

If you genuinely discover that you really do need to trash your personal values to rise to the top, this may be a career block (see **Chapter 10**), and a possible reason for moving on to another organization. Ultimately the organizational culture has the biggest effect, and the question facing many would-be senior staff is whether you can genuinely hope to change a culture or whether you will be beaten down in the attempt.

Ascending the slippery pole

Real career progression shouldn't be about the damage you do to other people in order to get to the top. If it is, life has a habit of biting you back. Shark-like behaviour works in the short term, but leaves you short of friends. It also does huge long-term damage to organizations, work colleagues, and to personal relationships.

Success should be about standing on the shoulders of giants, not clambering over others in a mad scramble to the top. And if you have any lingering doubts about the balance of ethics and results, take the long view. How many of the people who back-stab their way to the top have long-term friendships outside work, or relationships of trust in work? How many of them could go back to one of the organizations or people in their past and ask for help? It's unlikely that any of us will lie on our deathbed wishing we'd made more enemies.

WORKING OUT HOW OTHERS SEE YOU

Seen and unseen

When considering the impact you have on others, and how far you are able to communicate your strengths to an organization, it's important to know your limitations, and enlist the support of others. In marketing terms it's the difference between a new product that you think is a marvellous idea, and something that is tested among target purchasers.

The Johari window (see **Figure 6.1**) provides us with some insights into the difference between the way we see ourselves, and the way others see us.

The idea behind the Johari window is that we achieve personal growth by expanding area number 1. We can in fact only discover information in boxes 2 and 3 in relationship; by listening to others (2) and by disclosing to others (3). We can

	KNOWN TO MYSELF	UNKNOWN TO MYSELF
KNOWN TO OTHERS	**1 OPEN SELF** Aspects of yourself that your are aware of that are also perceived by others (the impression you know you are giving)	**2 BLIND SELF** Aspects of yourself that you are NOT aware of that are perceived by others (the impression you may be giving, unknown to yourself)
UNKNOWN TO OTHERS	**3 HIDDEN SELF** Aspects of yourself that you are aware of that are NOT perceived by others (the part of you that you hide)	**4 UNKNOWN SELF** Aspects of yourself that you are NOT aware of that are NOT perceived by others (unexplored aspect, hidden strengths and motivations)

Figure 6.1   The Johari window

only reach box 4 by reflection, and again this often works best when supported by others.

This tool is useful because it shows that employers and work colleagues may be making decisions about us based on information in 2 – attributes which are perceived by others, but not by you. You need to know if this is the case; this is one of the major benefits of feedback and appraisal – discovering exactly how others see you, and how that relates to your self-image.

Also you may discover that many of your strengths are hidden away in box 3 – you are aware of them, but others are not. This is the importance of self-disclosure, which in commercial terms comes back to the key issue: marketing yourself.

CHANGING THE WAYS OTHERS SEE YOU

This book has argued that your career really gets on track when you find a genuine trade-off between your goals and the current anxieties and vision of your employer. But you also need to know how to present your side of the working deal. As we have discovered, communicating yourself within an organization is essentially a piece of marketing – one that is most effective if you have a strong grasp of how you are seen already, and how you would like to change that perception. The following checklist rehearses different contexts for active marketing.

1. Reaching out to people

Successful workers are often those who have cultivated a wide range of contacts within the organization as information resources. You need a team of people who can assist you on your journey:

■ Trusted colleagues who can advise you on the way you are perceived by the organization.

■ Honest friends who can tell you about the way you look and sound (don't ignore surface essentials like dressing well, looking smart, sounding alert and sharp, writing and speaking without making major grammatical errors).

■ Contacts within the organization who can tell you the real agenda and the most desired outcomes.

■ Those in your company who know the key people: who to talk to, who can tell you what's going on.

■ Others who have access to key information and knowledge.

■ Colleagues with particular skills from whom you can learn.

■ Other successful performers: what can you learn from their behaviours?

■ The key people you need to influence and impress.

2. Formal one-to-one meetings with senior managers

Think carefully about one-to-one encounters with anyone who

is a key decision-maker. **Chapter 10** talks about the way you should use contact time with your boss very carefully. If you have the opportunity to discuss something or communicate information to someone even more senior, use that time even more imaginatively.

Remember that this may be the first time that this senior manager has heard your voice or seen what you can do. Up to now you may have just been a face or a name. The first impression you make here will be as important as the initial impact you might make in a job interview, except here the stakes could be even higher.

Think carefully about why you are there. Is it to ask a question, convey information, or put forward an idea? Are you looking for a view, or a decision? If your role here is essentially *input*, plan what you are going to say and go through it briefly and concisely. Back up your spoken words with written information. Be prepared to answer questions, but don't let them put you off communicating your main message. If you are seeking *output* from a senior manager, make it very clear from the outset what you are looking for: 'I'd like your view about ...' or 'I wonder if you can give me a decision on ...?'

Some warnings and reminders here:

▪ Make sure *your* boss is aware of the conversation beforehand if he or she might feel threatened or sidestepped by this conversation.

▪ Be clear what you want to get out of the interaction.

▪ Don't ask for information that you could have obtained from this manager's subordinate, or worse still from a document that is already on your PC.

▪ Confirm details in writing, if appropriate in a follow-up email or memo.

▪ Always fulfil, or over-fulfil, against anything you commit to during this meeting. If you don't, the manager will assume that you are unreliable in all aspects of your work performance.

3. Other one-to-one opportunities

You may discover many informal opportunities to interact with key decision-makers in your organization. Suddenly discovering the head of finance is next to you in the lunch queue, for example. You might bump into a senior member of staff in a social situation. You may be working side by side (possibly in roles of equal status) in a voluntary assignment.

When this happens don't assume that this manager will remember who you are and where you work. A reasonable good way is to say hello warmly, and quickly introduce yourself by name and function. What next? Be careful of anything that impinges on personal matters (even your director's choice of dessert!), but perhaps say something positive about her most recent press appearance or conference speech or article in the company newsletter. Don't let flattery become fawning, but it never harms to show that you're aware of someone's profile. The principle here is about putting yourself on the map, and increasing the awareness of key people. But tread carefully.

Should you engineer such an encounter? This is very much a matter for personal style – both yours, and the manager you are trying to meet. There have been successful approaches made through encounters that weren't quite chance – like knowing when someone is likely to take coffee or emerge from a lift. Keep it natural and relaxed – as soon as what you do looks calculated or obvious, or becomes repetitive, the greater the chances your contact will have the opposite effect to the one intended.

4. Your contribution to teams

Your contribution to teams gets noticed: both by people in those teams and those who hear reports of team activities.

Positive and negative behaviours in teams are most effective when they are new teams that mix staff from different departments. You're on stage in much the same way you will be when you make a public presentation (see below). If your contribution is positive and effective, it's highly likely that news of this will reach key decision-makers.

Generally it's best to keep cynicism under wraps. It's all too easy to accept the prevailing tone when others are running the company down, or – worse – criticizing key figures. Join in, and you never know how your words will be repeated. This could be a Career-Limiting Action (see **Chapter 10**).

Chapter 12 will give you the opportunity to identify your natural team role, and seek opportunities (particularly in cross-departmental teams or teams involving key players) to join and work with teams. Seek teams that form to undertake a particular project and then disband when the project is complete. Committees, on the other hand, have a life of their own and can tie you down to unproductive activity for years.

5. Relationships outside the organization

Chapter 11 gives you a great many tips on networking with key people outside your organization. What needs to be said here is that there are people outside your organization that you can influence in order to change the way your company sees you. These will include the contacts listed in **Table 6.2**.

PRESENTATIONS: THE KEY TO VISIBILITY

One of the most important means you have of influencing others is through the opportunities you have to make presentations. This is such an important topic the rest of this chapter is devoted to it. Why is it important? Because, as we discuss elsewhere, the decision to take you seriously as a player in the organization is often made around just two or three of your actions – and what is often remembered is the times when you

Table 6.2   Key marketing relationships outside your organization

■ **Customers** – being seen as the key link person into your organization. Customers buy people as much as products.

■ **Suppliers** – being given the opportunity to achieve KRAs by ensuring you attract the right resources a the right price.

■ It sometimes does no harm to your career if **competitors** see your strengths – at least it gives your company a strong reason to retain you.

■ Other **business relationships** – seek opportunities to represent your organization with trade associations, your local Business Link, local government and schools.

■ The local **community** – being seen as a representative or spokesperson for a company is usually role-enhancing.

■ **Recruiters** and **headhunters** – getting the odd enquiry or invitation to move on can be confidence-building, and can also give you the opportunity to keep your ear to the ground about what's going on.

---

did something in the public gaze. It's one obvious way that makes you visible and interesting, so it's the kind of event that will come up in conversations about your future.

Outplacement consultant Bernard Pearce found that this skill was critical in his own development: 'Learning to present information, ideas and concepts in a way that raises confidence and both motivates and inspires the listener. It is the ability to present well that separates the leaders from managers!'

The art of convincing presentations

Whether you're presenting to clients or colleagues, you need to know what you're doing. A good presentation to customers counts because everything you do and the way you do it is taken as an indication of supply standards.

Don't make the mistake of thinking that presentations to colleagues and superiors are any less important. In career terms, they matter first. Someone in that room may be making a decision about your next move just as you are speaking. Again, your presentation style and standard will – quite unreasonably – be taken as an indication of your total effectiveness within the organization.

Preparation

There is no such thing as too much preparation. Only the most experienced presenters can plan to wing it on the day. We watch consummate performers who appear to do everything off the cuff, and make the mistake of believing that it's all spontaneous. It isn't. Inspiration draws on experience and practice. The late comic genius Tommy Cooper's hallmark was an act that was a shambles, and always on the edge of chaos. Every stumbling moment was carefully rehearsed.

US Defence Secretary Colin Powell made a critical presentation to the United Nations in February 2003. Not only did he rehearse, write, and research his speech painstakingly, he delivered it several times in advance to colleagues. At one stage he had a room set up to replicate exactly the room where he would be speaking. Preparation makes the difference.

Planning to be successful

The key to success in presentations is beginning with the end in mind. Why are you presenting? What do you want to *happen* as a result of your talk? Do you need to make a presentation at all? There's nothing worse than listening to a 90-minute explanation of information that could be covered in a 10-line handout.

Run the movie

If you are nervous about presenting, here's a trick for stage fright which is learned by opera singers. Don't think about the initial moments of terror as you begin, but think about the final moment just after you finish: a delighted, appreciative audience. Then work backwards, visualizing your closing moments, then the substance of what you do, and finally get to the starting point in your head.

The reason this works is that the human brain finds it difficult to distinguish between actual and imagined experience. Athletes know this well: if you have a strong picture of hitting the finishing tape first, your brain reacts as if this is something you have actually done before, and seeks resources to help you do it again. If you visualize the best version of yourself making a presentation, and practice to reinforce effective skills, then by running the internal 'success movie' you will capture some of the same results as actually doing it.

Top and tail

Memorize your opening words so you know you will begin well. First impressions count, so don't cough, mumble or stumble over your first words. Stand straight, deliver your opening statement clearly and not too quickly – your audience is tuning in to your voice gradually and taking in a lot of other visual information about you, your dress style, your behaviours – so take it slow and steady. Look at people while you talk to them. Get a feeling for the mood and level of attention of the room. Memorizing a brief, strong closing statement works too. That way you know that if you get lost somewhere in the middle, you always have the lifeline of a great finish.

Design your material so you can cut it down if you end up with a shorter time that you planned, or if you are losing the audience's attention. They may have been bored by the last speaker!

Too much of presenting is about talking and telling. Top-performing sales people know that the best strategy is to ask rather than tell. Ask people what their concerns are, or the gaps in their understanding. Find out before you stand up and speak.

Filling the sandwich

The best presentations are short, sweet, and memorable. A politician only needs 4 minutes in a radio spot to get across her three main points of the day. Most people are only capable of holding about five pieces of information in their heads simultaneously, and prefer three. If you overinform, you clutter and confuse. Begin by deciding what three key messages you want to get across.

If you have complex supporting information like statistics or examples, use them sparingly. If you have detailed handouts, don't give them out until you have communicated your main points, because half your audience will be reading, not listening.

Beware the old adage repeated so often in books about public speaking: *tell them what you're going to tell them, tell them, tell them you've told them*. It's really dull. Be clear, and reinforce your point, but please don't say the same thing three times. Your audience is smarter than you think.

Use humour carefully, but use it if you dare – too many business talks are humourless. Make your word pictures as interesting as your visuals. And make sure that you finish on a clear, positive note – a question, a challenge, a statement. First and last words matter.

A 10-POINT PRESENTATION CHECKLIST

1. Stand up and walk to the lectern or end of the boardroom table as if you already have the audience's complete attention, and you will.

2. Try to have an opening statement or statistic that really catches your audience's attention. A phrase like 'Most advertising is a waste of time' usually does the trick.

3. Avoid reading from extensive notes. Use bulleted words or phrases if you need to. All you should need is about 6–10 cartoon images on a piece of card to remember the key themes in a 20-minute talk.

4. Use visual aids to complement what you say, not repeat it. Put only a small amount of text in PowerPoint slides.

5. Use more than just visual images. Physical props make great visual aids.

6. Vary your volume, tone and speed. Listen to professional speakers, and learn.

7. Look people in the eye when you tell them the important stuff. If you don't they won't believe you.

8. If you are quoting something short and powerful, pause, and repeat it.

9. Remember that about 80% of your message is in the way you dress, move, and in all the mannerisms that distract (or convince) your listener.

10. Strike the right balance between snappy and good value. You can always offer to expand at the end of your talk – if your audience wants to hear more, they will ask questions.

'MUST DO' LIST

☑ How are you communicating the idea that you are an asset and not just a cost to your employer?

☑ What first steps could you take to understand your organization's preferred style of self-marketing? Talk to people who have done it successfully – achieved what they wanted without trampling down others on the way.

☑ How do others see you in the organization? Take soundings from friends and colleagues. Don't seek flattery, but an honest answer to the question 'What do people think that I contribute?'

☑ Seek opportunities to present your message to key individuals and groups.

☑ Work on your presentation style. Begin with short, memorable presentations to small teams and colleagues, and work up to public presentations which get you noticed.

Thriving in
Difficult Times

This chapter helps you to:

▌ Understand the dangers of survivor mentality

▌ Learn what you can do to try to avoid redundancy

▌ Recognize the importance of 'political' awareness in a job

▌ Move from 'survive' to 'thrive'

By working faithfully 8 hours a day, you may eventually get to be a boss and work 12 hours a day.

Robert Frost

WORKING IN UNCERTAIN TIMES

Taking control of your career may sound like a luxury if you feel you're trying to hold down a job in a strong gale. It's difficult to see options and choices if you feel you're simply hanging on to the wreckage, and you feel you're simply in survivor mode.

Understanding survivor mentality

In her thoughtful book *Strike A New Career Deal*, Carole Pemberton recounts how workers who have managed to survive waves of redundancies and downsizing become focused on job security and lose sight of both their own personal goals and the aims of the organization. The survivor mindset is usually to keep your head down and keep your job. Ironically, this approach encourages behaviours that fail to endear you to managers: invisibility, conformity, an aversion to risk taking. Pemberton researched job 'survivors' and found that they adopted one of four strategies:

1. Getting ahead – continuing to seek career progression.

2. Getting 'safe' – protecting job security, seeing things out until retirement.

3. Getting out – which often involves jumping ship without any real thought or preparation.

4. Getting even – undermining change or actively sabotaging projects in the company.

(From Strike A New Career Deal, Carole Pemberton,
Financial Times/Prentice Hall, 1998)

If you feel you are in survivor mode you may feel negative about yourself and the opportunities available to you. Organizations often make the mistake of thinking that people who survive redundancy will feel so grateful to be retained that they will work harder. This is generally far from the truth. Demotivation and insecurity usually follow, along with a sense of guilt because we've kept our jobs while others haven't.

You can also find the survivor mindset in people who follow 'getting safe' thinking – keeping your head down, keeping out of the way of trouble. This might be a strategy that can work for you in the short term, but it's no way to live your working life. This behaviour almost guarantees that you are considered part of the dead wood of the organization.

Defence strategies to avoid being first on the redundancy list

Sometimes redundancy is unavoidable: if it's caused by external factors, or if there has been a huge downturn in your sector. Highly skilled, useful people are made redundant by organizations. Managers will also tell you that, unofficially, organizations get rid of people who aren't part of the main event – or at least don't give the impression that they are. People whose skills seem out of date, whose contribution to the organization seems lightweight – and people who just don't fit. Anything you can do to improve your profile in a positive way is an action that does something, no matter how small, to keep you off the redundancy list.

Do be aware, however, that being made redundant shouldn't be taken, in itself, as a reflection of your employability. Organizations 'let people go' for a wide variety of reasons, and don't always get rid of the right people. So, although it's important to have a strategy to present yourself as useful as possible to an organization, do also recognize that redundancy is a fact of life for a large proportion of workers, and if it happens to you then don't make the mistake of taking it personally.

However, it would be very negative just to stay in survival mode, grimly hanging on to your job. How much more positive to find ways of moving from safety to achievement? One of the ways of retaining your job is to act as positively as you can, and avoid Career-Limiting Actions. **Chapter 10** has more details. First, though, we need to check whether you are clinging to the wreckage in survivor mode because of difficulties working out where your career is going.

AVOIDING THE MINEFIELDS: HANDLING ORGANIZATIONAL POLITICS

What do we mean by organizational politics? Let's look at some of the descriptions used by perpetrators and victims. To those who enjoy politics, it's about competition, getting ahead, winning. To those who lose out because of internal politics, it's about deception, manoeuvring, and an unhealthy interest in making sure others don't succeed. Politics at work often causes confusion, a lack of shared objectives, and a failure to encourage talented workers. Ultimately it results in cynicism.

> Jill works for an organization where nothing can change unless a decision is made by one of the divisional heads. However, to gain access to the head of division, she needs to negotiate through their PAs. Two of these PAs are at loggerheads. If Jill goes to Manager A, Manager B's PA will cut her out of the loop. A huge amount of energy in the company goes into playing off one PA against another. A critical decision behind any action is which lobby you support, and which you choose to have as an enemy. Jill's experience is that great ideas get shot down simply because they are supported by the wrong faction.

How do you deal with the politics?

You might believe that the simplest method is to side with the strongest party. Doing that, however, means you play by house rules. It won't be long before you find yourself concealing information or telling half-truths. How long before you begin to relish others' misfortune? Look back at all the times when you have been complicit, perhaps in an unwitting way, perhaps because of good motives. When has your behaviour been manipulated? The first problem of playing organizational politics is that you only win by losing – by losing integrity, friends, and losing a belief in yourself. Very few people go into retirement wishing they had been more cunning at work. Some of them wish that they had more real friends.

So how do you survive in a politicized environment, when you're supposed to take sides, toe the party line, say which side you're on … ? **Table 7.1** offers a 20-point checklist for dealing with the politics inside an organization.

Table 7.1   20 steps to getting round organizational politics

1 **Be aware of the politicians.** That's more than being aware of your discomfort: you need to recognize the people who are the key influencers in the organization.

2 **Look at the damage.** It's often healthy and useful to help identify what goes wrong as a result of playing politics – the deals that are missed, the talent that leaves the organization. Discuss the downside with your colleagues.

3 **Watch your back.** Are you treading, inadvertently, on someone else's toes? Are you in somebody's way? Many honest, diligent people just don't see the knife coming in their back. Recruit or work alongside others who have better 'radar' than you.

4 **Draw your line in the sand.** Before the crunch comes, be clear about what you are not prepared to do to win.

5 **Be honest.** There really is no other policy, and you have to have a tremendous memory to tell lies in an organization. But remember that being honest doesn't give you *carte blanche* to criticize others. See **Step 6.**

6 **Praise or be silent.** Remember your mother's advice: 'if you can't say anything nice, don't say anything at all'. Try to find something positive to say about your colleagues, or keep your peace.

7 **Avoid gossip.** OK, it's fun, but be careful to spot the line between discreet observations and character assassination. Distance yourself from 'toxic' attitudes and people.

8 **Find allies and avoid enemies.** It helps to have people on your side, but recruit them by helping them, providing useful information, and showing you do a great job.

9 **Identify the politics-free zones.** There are usually some key managers or decision-makers in organizations who manage to bypass the cutting and thrusting. Get them on your side, and follow their strategies.

10 **Check how far your success means someone else's failure.** Getting ahead requires competition, but doesn't have to cause someone else's downfall.

11 **Accentuate the positive.** You may find yourself surrounded by negative comments and thinking. It sometimes takes only a small effort to encourage people to see the glass as half full rather than half empty.

12 **Move out of cynical teams.** Cynical teams achieve very little, because they start from the position that it's all been tried before and there's no point anyway. If you're in a team like this and **Step 9** fails, try independent activity.

13 **Seek WIN/WIN.** Even in a highly politicized environment, it's possible to offer solutions that are a genuine win for both parties.

14 **Be consistent.** It's no use having integrity one day and being a conniving manipulator the next.

15 **Do what you say you will do.** Try it; it gets results. Fail to deliver (without explanation) and everything you say becomes an empty promise.

16 **Set 10% of your time aside to help others.** Consider this time well invested, and do it because you can, not because of any leverage it gives you.

17 **Help your boss win gracefully.** Make your boss look good – but not at the expense of making someone else look bad.

18 **Keep integrity as your surprise card.** You know what 'integrity' means to you. Stick to your principles, and don't dilute them. You may be the only person being straight and honest in your organization; if that's true, you are its greatest asset! Often the honest, non-manipulative strategy is the one that surprises.

19 **Lose gracefully.** If others jump the queue, push you aside or outmanoeuvre you, don't be tempted to play by the same rules. He who lives by the sword … .

20 **Consider moving on.** Don't use your failure to handle the politics as a stick to beat yourself. Organizational politics are hard to manage, even for the best operators. If you can't find a way to handle it, can't find the right allies, and your personal integrity is threatened too often, it may be time to move out. And when you do, don't let your message to your next employer be about the damage the organization has done to you.

When someone is making your life hell at work

As an employee you have the legal right to enjoy a workplace that is free from bullying or victimization. If you are on the receiving end of this kind of behaviour, take advice. It may not always be effective to make a formal complaint immediately – test the water first by discussing the problem with senior staff without making it official. An quiet word is will often solve a problem. It's worth thinking about the *outcome* you have in mind – do you want retribution, or simply the opportunity to get on with your job? Sometimes it's better for your health to walk away from these battles.

Many situations are irritatingly intangible: life is being made uncomfortable for you, but there is no solid evidence; perhaps you're being set up to ensure that you fail, or given what the British Army calls 'all assistance short of actual help'.

The first step is to tell the difference between things you can do something about, and things that are outside your control. **Table 7.2** offers some ground rules, but refer back to **Chapter 6** for more on aggressive self-promoters.

TAKE CONTROL AND THRIVE IN DIFFICULT TIMES

In order to move on from survivor mode to a position where you are beginning to thrive, you need to learn how to look in new ways at your job and go beyond the boundaries of your job description. You will also need to develop a double perspective on what you do: looking outside the organization at changes in your field of work, and also looking back inside the organization to understand how other people see you.

Get a new perspective on your job

A great interim step is to take what marketing specialist Philip Spencer calls an 'outside in' view of your company. Essentially,

Table 7.2   Dealing with manipulative behaviours in the workplace

■ Often manipulative behaviour is prompted by fear. Look at what you might be doing that is threatening someone else's position. Make it as clear as you can that you are not a threat.

■ If you have to deal with difficult behaviours, focus on the behaviour, not the person. Saying 'I felt uncomfortable when you criticized my idea' is far less challenging than 'you're a negative person'.

■ Co-operate rather than compete, even if the ground rules suggest that competition is the only option. Sometimes workplace values can be shifted by not conforming with the dominant negative feeling.

■ Make sure that you are helpful to all your colleagues, not just the ones who can help you get somewhere.

■ Avoid making critical remarks about colleagues, even if they seem out to get you. You never know how your words will be passed on. Saying nothing is a far easier position to defend.

■ If you have something better to offer than your colleagues, put the focus on your offer rather than on ways of making yourself look better than others.

■ Don't take it personally. You're not the first or the last person to be treated this way.

■ Don't seek revenge. If you do, you've just been manipulated into playing by a whole new set of rules.

this is about looking at your job from the perspective of an outsider. Is your contribution to the company clear? Would an outside observer see and value your contribution? Secondly, how does the work you do relate to the kind of work done by other people in other organizations? How is that work valued (salary, status, resources and so on)?

Look at the way your company brings in outside expertise, either in terms of consultants or other suppliers. If you can fill the gap, why are they ignoring you? It could be because no one has challenged the idea that the best talent likes outside the organization, or it could be that your 'offer' is seen as weak compared with outsiders.

Expand on your job description

Think of your job description as a starting point rather than a destination.

How elastic is your job? How far are you boxed in by your job description? If you think your job can't be altered or expanded, is this a restriction in the job, the organization, or your mindset? How could you add maximum value to your organization by making the smallest changes to your job?

Here's how Penny Beazley of Mossop Cornelissen & Associates in Toronto sees it: 'Broaden your horizons within the organization. Start networking (offer to be part of a project or task team, lunch with them, etc.) with people in other departments (particularly those of influence and key customers and suppliers if possible). Find out how the position that you are aiming for links with these internal and external stakeholders and how that may change. Try to identify what is key to developing and sustaining a good relationship with these stakeholders, but finding out what is important for *them* to succeed and how you can support their success.'

Keeping alert to changes in the world of work

Career awareness, as defined in **Chapter 3**, requires a mix of information: about you, about the employers you would like to work with, and about the changing world of work.

Having looked at the main internal constraints to progress, it's equally powerful to look outside the organization. **Chapter 5** helped you to gain a great awareness of the relative strengths and weaknesses of your company, but the difference between survival and growth may depend on your ability to understand the fast-changing nature of the wider marketplace.

We all know how dangerous it is to try to predict the future workplace, but it's important to try. How well can you predict what your job will be like in 5 years' time? The bursting of the dot.com bubble meant that the markets suddenly lost faith in technology, but it hasn't gone away: every year computers get cheaper and more powerful. There are devices already in production that seem like pure science fiction. Some may fail to catch on, others could completely revolutionize the way we work. Let's look at two simple examples.

Travellers in the underground railways of Tokyo find the carriages so crowded it's impossible to read a newspaper. Now they can buy a pair of spectacles where one lens is converted to a mini-projector capable of displaying web pages. We are close to the point where we will be able to wear computer terminals as glasses or watches. How far away is the intelligent contact lens? And if you can access several million databases by blinking, what does that do to any job that involves communication or research?

Secondly, we're used to a range of handheld electronic devices, phones, laptops and personal organizers that can download email, text and even videos. The next generation of chips will be small and cheap enough to embed in items of clothing, and smart enough to communicate with each other using human skin as a connecting medium.

The combination of changing work patterns and cheap technology has brought about a number of important trends (see **Table 7.3**). How many of them are relevant to your job? What trends should you actively monitor? What are the trends that will give you an advantage?

Table 7.3 Work trends

Where work is done	Data processing, banking services and call centres have all recently been transposed to low-cost environments. There has been a huge increase, for example, in call centres in India. Entire manufacturing plants have been transposed from the USA and UK to China and other developing countries. As technology becomes cheaper, many more service industries will follow.
How work is done	The UK has predicted a huge increase in homeworking for some years. This hasn't yet had the predicted impact – possibly because of the social benefits of actually attending a workplace. This may change quickly, particularly if road congestion increases or fuel costs rocket.
Who does the work?	As the workforce ages and travel problems continue (e.g. gridlocked motorways and air travel delayed by long security processes), time becomes the most important commodity. We already seek to find ways of delegating our home tasks (ironing, walking the dog, childminding, etc.), and it's likely that we will follow the same strategy with work activities (avoid those dreary book-keeping tasks by delegating them online to someone the other side of the world?).
How will people be employed?	The last two decades have already seen a real flexing of categories: employed, fixed-term contracts, sub-contractors, temps, interim managers, consultants, associates, etc. It seems likely that we will see far more of this fragmentation, far

	more 'portfolio' careers, and more occasions where we negotiate the parameters of our relationship with an employer.
What experience will be considered valuable?	21st century employers have already redefined the ideal skills profile several times. As technical skills are automated, interpersonal skills become ever more important. Secondly, organizations change so fast that they need people with excellent change and project management skills.
What roles are most likely to change?	Essentially, any functional jobs that can be done online (producing communications, processing accounts, handling distribution, etc.) will move into low-cost regions. As a result, the jobs that remain in the developed world will either be 'high touch' (with highly developed interpersonal skills), immediate (you can't get your dustbin emptied online) or complex (calling on know-how, specialist knowledge, and face-to-face consultation). As we value our leisure time increasingly, it seems likely that the 'high-touch' area will continue to include a wide range of personal services from shopping assistants to cocktail mixers.
The demise of traditional career routes	Predictions suggest that most of us will experience not just regular job change, but possibly three or four changes of occupational field during a working lifetime. The skills and mindset you begin your career with won't be the set you finish with.

Understand why perceptions matter

Look at the people who fast track their way up the ladder in organizations. Are they always the most skilled? The most meticulous when it comes to looking after customers? The best at achieving targets? Sometimes, but more often it is not the true performers on an objective scale, but the people who *appear* to be doing the right things.

For Stuart McIntosh of CMC the critical question is 'Are you visible to and positively perceived by all the major stakeholders who will have an influence on your career?'

The cynics usually mumble at this point about toadying your way up the slippery slope, about spin-doctors and self-publicists. Well, a great deal of that goes on as well, but few long-term careers are built on such shaky foundations, largely because people need very good memories to remember the lies they told last week. You can't fool all the people all of the time.

Carole Pemberton, author and founder of Career Matters, suggests that 'much of our success is down to how others see us against the demands which they are facing, and whether we are on their radar. To talk of *image* can make selection choices seem superficial, but the truth is we all create images of others within work, e.g. risk-taker, reliable, innovator, inflexible, influencer, deliverer. Career success comes from identifying what your image is and then looking to make it work within the prevailing context. Just as people talk about situational leadership where leaders need different styles for different situations, there are situational careers. Your career can flourish in one situation because there is a good match between you and the context and decline when that context changes.'

In reality, being 'in the right place at the right time' is about *perception*, which can be a matter of accident, but is far more commonly a matter of conscious or unconscious design, as **Table 7.4** makes clear.

Table 7.4   How do you position yourself?

Unconscious positioning	Conscious positioning
Your boss happens to notice you handle a difficult customer well	You share with your boss what you learned about dealing with the difficult customer, and ask her advice about doing it even better next time.
You cover someone else's work	You use the chance to meet new people and ask questions about how another area of work is done.
You learn new skills in your own time	You seek to apply new skills by seeking opportunities to try out new activities at work that will benefit you employer.
You do something beyond the call of duty	You record and pass on customer feedback. You also pass on the successful techniques that achieved you the good feedback.
You dislike public praise	You seek one-to-one feedback on how you can improve, and seek opportunities to share your techniques with others.
You perform tasks to an excellent standard, and you're aware of the short cuts to success.	You share your expertise with others by passing on tips and insights. You are given the chance to train or coach others.

WORK DEPENDENCY

Once you've looked at the way others perceive your contribution at work, it's worth looking again at your relationship with your employer. How dependent are you on your job? How threatened would you feel if you lost your job or your role changed dramatically? Look at **Table 7.5** to see where you fit into the Work Dependency Scale.

TABLE 7.5 Work Dependency Scale

Depth of relationship	Degree of dependency	What you get out of work
Free spirit		
You move in and out of organizations at your ease, never putting all your eggs in once basket. You feel in control of your working time and the time you give to other life activities.	Work has variety, and you quickly gain experience of a range of work cultures. Likely to appeal to you if you have a strong sense of independence.	You may have to cope with low job security, and there may be times when you're not working. You may also become over-stretched. Some employers may find you a little too unconventional for a permanent job.
Committed individualist		
You give a huge amount to work, but you don't depend on it to press all your buttons. You don't plan to move on in a hurry, and certainly not without making a significant contribution. You're committed, but no doormat.	It's important to think how you are going to differentiate yourself from the **free spirit** and the **dependent activist**, otherwise your distinctive role may not be noticed. It's too easy for your contribution to the organization to go unnoticed if you don't make the effort to communicate your strengths.	You look and sound like a key player, which gets you noticed. However, you won't be taken for granted, as your colleagues will see you clearly have market value and you won't be around for ever if nothing changes.

Dependent activist

A huge amount of you is invested in work: your self-esteem, your status. You work long hours and you're always looking for new tasks. You don't take your holiday allowance.

You may not recognize the cost of your dependency. Work is fun, but it may be taking up so much of your life that there is no room left for relationships. What happens to you when this job comes to an end? Who will you talk to the day after you retire?

You get a buzz out of work, and you're probably seen as a key player. You may be next in line for promotion, although there is a risk that your employer will take you for granted as your enthusiasm is always on tap, and you're clearly eager to stay in the job.

Bonded servant

You're probably watching the clock and spend a great deal of time wishing you were somewhere else. However, you feel underskilled and in a difficult market, so you feel totally dependent on your employer.

Work is predictable, with few surprises, and at least you can switch off at five o'clock and do something more exciting. There is always a degree of resentment; you will easily fall into victim mode, blaming the job for your lack of health, wealth and fun.

You dislike your job and feel trapped by it. You feel you have little control over your working life. Your dissatisfaction with your job probably spills over into other parts of your life.

For some, the relationship is light and they are closest to being **free spirits**. It's sometimes true for older workers – they feel they have done the conventional career things and are happy to have a looser, less committed working arrangement. Occasionally this is the mindset adopted by those who have suffered redundancy more than once – a sense of caution, perhaps, before tying the knot once again .... **Free spirits** often have a relaxed approach to employment relationships: 'something else will come along'. Sometimes this makes them a little too passive.

All this implies that the **free spirit** approach to work arises for negative reasons. For some, the 'easy come, easy go' approach is a comfortable way of life. If not this job, then another is easily found. This is often true of workers in their twenties who feel confident about the transferability of their skills.

The **committed individualist** is more common: they show commitment without seriously compromising their integrity or individualism. They will usually be fairly tuned in to what recruiters see as the industry norm for the right length of time to stay in a job.

For others, the relationship becomes closer to dependency. This can be for benign reasons: work provides everything they need: social interaction, self-esteem, challenges and rewards. In the **dependent activist** mode you find people who really do believe that hard work is always valued. They will often be the first to arrive and the last to leave, and the loss of employment for such people will be a real shock. They don't like to admit it, but they do feel as if they are irreplaceable. Retirement, or a switch to a less active working life, will often be a real strain.

The **bonded servant** is easy to spot. Usually downbeat about work, even if it's dressed up in irony. Usually looking for ways to get through the working day without too many snags. Hooked on work, but for all the wrong reasons. Like co-dependency in a marriage, this is a relationship that has many negative characteristics but there are always just enough reasons to keep things going. However the **dependent servant** is usually the first one on the redundancy list, and the last to be offered new projects.

Looking at your degree of work dependency will reveal many useful things: what you really get out of work, and how far you are locked in to a job that may not be giving you what you need.

'MUST DO' LIST

☑ What are you actively doing to be seen as the last candidate for redundancy?

☑ Where do you fit on the Work Dependency Scale?

☑ How are you positioned in your company? What's the first personal quality people think of when your name is mentioned?

☑ Are the politics in your organization getting in the way? If so, what can you do about it?

☑ What can you do to push the boundaries in your job?

Work vs Life

This chapter helps you to:

▌ Fit work into your life in a more balanced way

▌ Working out your life priorities

▌ Understand where you sit on your personal learning curve

▌ Consider taking a career break

▌ Explore an experimental approach to switching occupations

▌ Investigate retraining

The pitcher cries for water to carry and a person for work that is real.

Marge Piercy (from 'Circles on the Water')

INTEGRATING LIFE AND WORK

Working to goals that are bigger than work

Many people say they are looking for a more stimulating job, but they are confused about what they want to get out of work and life. In its strongest manifestation this may be some kind of career crisis. This can be precipitated by redundancy, by a personality clash at work, or by rejection from the job market. For most it's a sense of unease. My clients ask questions about what they have to offer and what the market is like, but the underlying puzzle seems to be 'What is my work really for?' Sometimes it's vital to take this question seriously.

Increasing your self-awareness allows you to look at your immediate environment, your employer, and at your marketplace, so you can negotiate, create or find the right opportunity. In all probability this means dealing with linked issues: learning, life balance, a career break, or changing your job completely.

The meaning of work seems to become increasingly important to us as we get older. It relates closely to what the psychologist Carl Jung called *individuation*. Individuation is a complex process that affects each of us differently, but it's essentially a time when we review what life is about. This new perspective on life can sometimes be the anxiety of a mid-life crisis, for others it may be a calm maturity. It's a time when we can become more comfortable with who we are, and less concerned about impressing others. It's common for time itself to be the main reason (a sense of mortality), but a range of life events can prompt these feelings, including divorce, redundancy, or health problems. Another common prompt is a bereavement, particularly the loss of one or both parents.

The idea of individuation springs from the work of Carl Jung, who argued that many people undergo a major transition or midlife crisis between our late thirties and mid-fifties. Our earlier life, he believed, is a time when we are preoccupied with establishing ourselves in the world, and with the desire to fulfil the goals that stem from our biological urges. In later life we begin to see the finiteness of our existence and become more concerned with realizing our core personal, spiritual and even religious values. We individuate or find our way through the mass of competing motivations and desires to a more whole sense of purpose and self, and in recognizing our true values we may well leave behind some the of the purposes, goals and activities of an earlier time, because they no longer satisfy us or even seem meaningful. This can obviously have an impact on our feelings regarding the career we have chosen. It may mean we become disenchanted or burned out, or we may seek to find some new way of expressing our core values in a way that displaces our career path.

If this process is resolved successfully, the individuated self will tend to regain the capacity to see life positively. Where individuation is unsuccessful, it may cause continued unhappiness and a sense of being at odds with life. In the longer term, the individuated self is able to approach old age, and ultimately death, with an increasing sense of psychological wholeness or completeness.

Stuart Robertson, Occupational Psychologist

What is true for most people experiencing individuation is that we look at our past and try to make sense of it, and we feel the need to make important decisions about how we spend the rest of our working life. In the words of the great 1950s song, we wake up one morning and say *Is that all there is?*

Integrity in work

Bill Walmsley, Business Development Director of CERTT, reminds you to 'Be true to yourself – it's no fun getting promoted and finding yourself a square peg in a round hole.'

Increasingly we're not just thinking about career progression (moving from up the ladder rung by rung) but *career enhancement* – finding a way of allowing work to enrich more parts of your life than your wallet. Career enhancement is about working out what *you* have to offer and communicating that the best way you can, and so it certainly shouldn't be about becoming somebody different. As the discussion on individuation above makes clear, our ultimate goal might be about living a complete life – a career of integrity. Integrity is a perfect word here, because it captures a sense of doing things that are true to the way we are, and a sense of wholeness and well-being.

Promises, promises: is there life after work?

We've reached a point where we need to find a useful way of thinking about the work/life balance.

Much has been written on this subject in recent years. Very often we are made to feel that there is an ideal work/life balance. This can easily become one more reason to beat yourself up: *my life balance is wrong*. What matters is what balance you think is important to you (and to your growth and well-being) and your family, and then take an objective look at where your time is actually spent. Sometimes you have to live with the things you don't or can't do, but then work actively to improve the margins of your life where you have some influence.

> Behind some parental compulsion to bring home exaggerated amounts of pay is often a flight from the joy of living life here and now in the family – as if the future were more important than the present. ... *We ought not to postpone living because of work or because of our plans for buying something with the money we make.*
>
> (Matthew Fox, *The Reinvention of Work*,
> Harper Collins, 1994)

Many people talk about the things they would like to do with their life, but they are rarely asked how they would like to quantify these activities. Try it this way. If you think that you would like to do something for, say, at least one day a month, then you might try to block out one day in your diary and ring fence it. Alternatively, you might work out what that would mean in terms of time in a typical week. One 8-hour day a month translates into roughly 2 hours a week, or about

25 minutes a day during the working week. Even assuming you are only 50% successful, very few of us can really fail to find 12 minutes a day to do something you've been promising yourself for years. Perhaps you want to improve your conversational Italian? Twelve minutes a day, every day, will dramatically increase your vocabulary.

> I have taken steps to achieve balance between my career(s) and the other things in my life. Working from home where no one but you is responsible for how you allocate your time does require certain skills, including organization, planning and time management. I have found that it helps to be very disciplined. For example, I create a break between my home as my home and my home as my office by going down the road to a café every morning. I keep this break between home and work even when friends phone. My friends have had to be trained to understand that when I say I work from home I really mean I 'work' and cannot chat endlessly just because the network in their office has crashed and they can't do any work. At the end of the working day I will walk out of my study and turn off the computer and do other things. If I'm seeing a client in the evening then I may well take some compensating time out in the afternoon as 'time for me'.
>
> Halik Kochanski, Career Coach

You may feel that your goals can't be achieved in small bursts of activity. For example, it's difficult to pick up a complex skill in such short bursts. And what if your priority activity is, for example, taking longer holidays with your partner. However these 12 minutes a day can also be used for planning or just even *thinking* – to enable you to create the time that matters.

'Take time to know and appreciate the things in life that matter to you', recommends Lynda Pickess, Sales Director of Manpower UK, 'make sure you continue to ensure that these feature in your life.' The important thing is that you distinguish between the ideal and the real: not just what you'd like to do, but what you *will do*. This is a principle that applies not only to work objectives but to life goals – how much longer are you going to put off the things that really matter to you? And how can you integrate these goals into having a successful career? The answers are sometimes complicated, often unacceptable – but require a strong focus on the overall balance of your life.

Here's one practical strategy from David Podger, Commercial Director of Hawksmere Ltd: 'I "overlap" activities, i.e. I serve on the board of a not-for-profit organization where I can use my professional expertise in a different setting – and with different people. I travel only when absolutely necessary and try to spend as little time away from home as possible. I start late so I can take my children to school in the morning. I block out parents evenings/other personal commitments in my diary as non-specific "appointments" and don't change them.'

Another useful perspective comes from executive recruiter Andrew Tallents, who found a huge difference between 'a culture where all work and no play was encouraged' and 'a culture that encouraged a balance work/home life. I now have a great job working with people I like where the culture rewards delivery against objectives rather than the number of hours you put into the business. I am not necessarily working any less hard but I am in more control of my time which means I choose whether to see my daughter play for the school netball team rather than working.'

EXERCISE 8.1 – LIFE PRIORITIES

Reflecting on your life balance isn't about juggling your diary, but thinking about what work adds to life, and detracts from it. Complete **Table 8.1** below to work out what activities outside paid employment are important to you, thinking about both time for yourself and time for others.

Table 8.1 Life priorities

Read through the checklist of activities below and tick the appropriate box. Some may be things you do frequently, others may be things you do rarely. NOTE: Your time may be filled with activities which are 'important' to other people (e.g. caring for a sick relative). For this exercise, focus on the activities that are important and enjoyable for *you*.

If there are any activities you wish to add, include them at the bottom of the table.

	1 NOT important to me and NOT enjoyable	2 Important to me but NOT enjoyable	3 NOT Important to me BUT enjoyable	4 Important to me AND enjoyable	5 Very important to me AND enjoyable/ valuable to my life
Working for yourself (paid or unpaid work you do for interest)					
Quiet time with friends and family					
Playing with children					
Socializing with friends					

Table 8.1 (Contd)

	1 NOT important to me and NOT enjoyable	2 Important to me but NOT enjoyable	3 NOT Important to me BUT enjoyable	4 Important to me AND enjoyable	5 Very important to me AND enjoyable/ valuable to my life
Listening to or playing music, singing, dancing					
Painting, drawing, being artistic					
Writing for pleasure or reflection					
Theatre, or concerts,					
Watching Movies					
Relaxing on my own					
Reading for pleasure					
Gardening					

Table 8.1 (Contd)

	1 NOT important to me and NOT enjoyable	2 Important to me but NOT enjoyable	3 NOT Important to me BUT enjoyable	4 Important to me AND enjoyable	5 Very important to me AND enjoyable/ valuable to my life
Home improvement or decorating					
Being trained or learning on the job					
Studying in my own time					
Going on courses					
Reflecting/thinking/ meditating					
Looking after others					
Food shopping, cleaning					
Preparing meals					
Keeping fit, enjoying sport					

Table 8.1 (Contd)

	1 NOT important to me and NOT enjoyable	2 Important to me but NOT enjoyable	3 NOT Important to me BUT enjoyable	4 Important to me AND enjoyable	5 Very important to me AND enjoyable/ valuable to my life
Walking					
Having health treatments, promoting my well-being					
Shopping for fun					
Making things with my hands					
Pet care					
Voluntary work for your community					
Worship, religious activity					
Other					

EXERCISE 8.2 – LIFE BALANCE

To complete this second half of the life balance exercise you need to work out roughly how much time you spend on each activity per week. If it is an occasional activity, make a rough estimate of how many hours you spend on it in a month, and then divide by four.

1. Look at the choices you have put in column 5 of **Table 8.1**.

2. Choose the **eight activities** that matter to you most, and write them out in the eight boxes in **Figure 8.1** below.

3. Now work out how much time you actually spend on each activity, shading in the appropriate number of rings out from the centre, using the time key as your guide. For example, you might label one box 'voluntary work' if this is a preferred activity. If you know that you commit about 2 hours a week to this, shade in the segments as far as ring 3.

4. When you have finished, look at the overall circle. Where are the blanks?

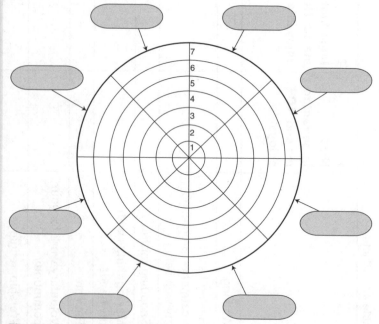

Figure 8.1   Life balance chart

Table 8.2 Life balance chart

Time key

1 Rarely: 15 minutes per week or less, possibly almost never

2 Occasionally: 30 minutes per week, possibly

3 Fairly regularly: maybe 1 hour a week or so

4 Regularly: 2 hours a week or so

5 Frequently: maybe 5 hours a week

6 Most days: 10 hours a week or more

7 Most of the time: 35 hours a week or more

CHOICES, CHOICES ...

Where is your career is taking you – and is it a direction you want to follow? Who's doing the driving? It's questions like this which ultimately make us reflect on the part work plays in our lives. It's important to ask the question: who judges the value of your career? Many of us measure career success against organizational benchmarks and the opinions of colleagues. Others decide what is important for themselves: time for children or grandchildren, or the opportunity to fulfil particular goals while we still have the health and energy. This shift in priorities may also prompt us to think about sabbatical leave or career breaks, and about the widest range of choices available.

Work has to be framed within the larger context of a life worth living.

Senior NHS Executive Val Michej suggests that you think about what you mean by success: 'I had time to reflect on how far I had defined myself through work, through the job I did. I came to understand that "success" is not only how you define it personally but how other people define it as well. If they define you as successful it means you probably are. There are may ways in which you can be successful. You don't have to be at the very pinnacle of an organization or profession or career, or even halfway there, to be valued as a role model for others, to support others to do the best they can, or to do your job to the best of your ability (and preferably better than anyone else!). And maybe you don't have to expend all your energy into your work, into the next big job, into the next promotion, but find time for all the other things that help define you as the unique and successful human being that you are.'

Being aware of your position on the learning curve

To begin thinking about life choices, you probably want to start by asking how much your job feeds you. One of the most common motivators is the ability to try out new things and to keep on learning in a job which offers some variety.

Every job has its own learning curve. When we talk about a 'steep learning curve' we describe a demanding but stimulating point in life when we are learning new skills and strategies, and learning them quickly. A slow learning curve implies either that you are taking a long time to make progress, or the job changes very slowly.

What both employers and workers fail to recognize, however, is that a learning curve has an ending as well as a beginning. When you have learned pretty much everything the job has to offer, and you no longer find tasks challenging or sufficiently varied, you've reached the top of the curve. This is often a point of career dissatisfaction. Sadly, many respond by seeking an alternative job for more money, placing themselves almost exactly at the same point on the learning curve.

As **Figure 8.2** shows, what happens at the top end of the learning curve matters. The curve can go in one of three directions. It can continue upwards, effectively moving into a new curve by offering new opportunities to grow and develop. It can (and often does) level out, meaning that staff continually have to

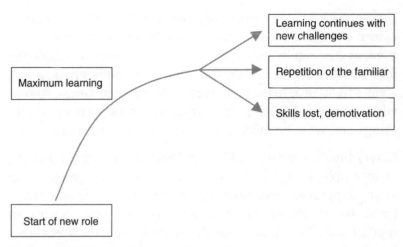

Figure 8.2   Possible directions of the learning curve

find new ways of motivating themselves, but often complain that work is the 'same old, same old'. This sometimes happens when work is done on an annual cycle, and while the first two or three years are exciting, eventually the work becomes repetitive. Or, more negatively still, it can fall away – when this happens you hear colleagues talking about being under-used or de-skilled.

Managers have a responsibility to monitor the point when staff reach the top end of the curve, but they are often too busy to do so. So it's up to you to learn one of the most powerful skills of the modern workplace: to monitor and manage your own learning.

Career breaks

It seems increasingly common to hear people talking about taking a career break (see the very useful *The Career Break Book* by Joe Bindloss, Clare Hargreaves and Charlotte Hindle, Lonely Planet Publications, 2005).

Some employers still give their staff sabbatical leave – to study, to travel, to refresh themselves. These breaks sometimes send people back to work renewed, and at other times prompt a career change. Sabbatical leave will be for a fixed period of time, and is usually only offered if you have been an employee for a number of years. There are sometimes conditions attached – you might have to make a case for taking a sabbatical, stating what you will be doing (e.g. researching or learning something) and what benefits it will bring the organization.

Career breaks are rather different. Usually they are not funded by an employer, although an enlightened employer might keep your job open for you. However, for many, the idea of a career break (taken out of choice rather than necessity) seems an unaffordable luxury, or a pipe dream. In some industries career breaks and sabbaticals are commonplace, in others unheard of.

The idea has roots far older than our present civilization. The Judao-Christian tradition of the Sabbath reflects the idea that all work needs to pause, and all workers need to recharge their batteries. The 24/7 economy increasingly reduces the time we have to do this. The need for breaks is more important than ever. Ultimately, it's about your choices, and your overall balance of learning, living, and working. However, it's important to include the idea of career breaks as part of the larger questions about why you want to be promoted, and how you want to spend your working life. When it comes to negotiating your 'offer' with your employer, past or future, remember that the time when you are not working can become part of the deal – time for doing more of the things you outlined in the work/life balance **Exercise 8.1** earlier.

Changing expectations

We're all becoming more tuned in to the idea that we may change not just jobs, but job sectors – and several times during a working lifetime. Some of us expect to change career between three and five times in a working lifetime – particularly those under the age of 30. In fact, there are those who argue very strongly that we only have one 'career', but it has different dimensions to it (including learning, career breaks, and family time), for example careers researcher Sara Bosley: 'By career I mean a sequence of jobs and job-related experiences, rather than the more commonly used meaning which implies increasing responsibility, status and income.'

'Fringe' working, as discussed in **Chapter 1**, becomes attractive at certain stages in life – often when you're experimenting your way through a career. It's common for people to experiment with career change during their twenties (for example, by taking temporary assignments to ease yourself into an industry). Later you may experiment yourself out of a conventional career by exploring work and life choices.

If you're looking at the part work plays in your life, one of the choices that will present itself to you is the idea of changing occupations. For many the idea of changing to a completely different field of work seems to be the answer to all of life's problems. This needs approaching with some caution. For one thing, you may have a distorted picture of other occupations. They, too, have their problems. Secondly, you may be looking for an exit route before you have really looked at what you are looking for in work.

However it's true that career shifts may happen for a number of different reasons:

▌ moving into a less-pressurized role

▌ moving into a role that is less under the control and direction of others

▌ moving into a role that avoids the complexity of organizational politics, committees, etc.

▌ finding work that is more directly meaningful and fulfilling

▌ moving into an occupation or field that is intrinsically more interesting

▌ moving into work that is connected with your personal interests, for example, turning a hobby into an occupation

If you're thinking about shifting occupations, it's important to register that it's tricky to change your sector of work *and* your occupation at the same time. For example, a primary school teacher may move from primary to secondary education, staying in the same occupation and roughly the same field. It's fairly frequent that qualified teachers become trainers or lecturers, retaining occupation but changing their field. It's harder to make a shift of both field and occupation, for example, a teacher becoming a sales representative.

This fact often puts people off, but a positive approach is to think of change as a series of stepping stones. Step one might be to find a job similar to the one you do now, but in another field of work. Take your project management, computer, or finance skills, for example, to a different field. To make this kind of move you will need to be good at demonstrating your transferable skills – don't assume that these will be understood unless you know how to explain them to a new employer. The second kind of stepping stone move is to do something different but stay in the sector that you know well. This often presents a win/win for employers as they get to retain your knowledge.

The reality is that most of us will experience a career shift at least once: a move to a different role or a different field. We're all more conscious of the possibility that a career may involve at least one occupational shift, and probably involves some retraining or new learning. We have choices to make, and the more aware we can become, the better our decisions in terms of investing in ourselves and choosing what to do next.

Experiment or leap?

You might have picked up this book or *How To Get A Job You'll Love* with the idea that hidden within you is 'real' person – a secret self that can be unlocked by asking the right questions or reading the right books. Many self-help books are written along these lines. What this encourages is a sense that if you discover your secret self, you discover the one, single career pathway that you should have followed.

It may be attractive to believe that you have a single, concealed 'dream' career, rather like the Monty Python accountant who always wanted to be a lumberjack. Occasionally you do meet people who have a very clear dream job. Many feel as if they *ought* to have an ideal job, and envy those who do – without realizing how demanding life is for those people who know that they really only have one choice if they want to avoid saying 'I wish …' for the rest of their lives.

The vast majority of us have a much more undefined sense of what we would 'really' like to do. For some, the lack of definition provides a great excuse – to do nothing. We're trained by our upbringing to seek clear outcomes and work hard at achieving them. We're not very good at 'What if?'.

The idea of multiple career routes helps, because instead of having one fixed idea you have a cluster of related possibilities. Now you're closer to career awareness (see **Chapter 3**).

Let's take Daniel as an example. He has spent all his career so far in accountancy roles, and now he is juggling a number of career ideas including charity work, public sector work for a housing association, working as a small business advisor, while he is at the same time very attracted by a commercial role in a large company. How does Daniel make sense of his options? Does he need to make a move? One answer to this question is for Daniel to make more of the **exploration zone** in his job (see **Table 4.2**), which is what he did. He created time to meet people in some of the work sectors that interested him. He persuaded his company to allow him to work much more closely with senior operations staff to get a 'feel' for the cutting edge of the business. Outside work he is working as a voluntary small business adviser with the Prince's Trust, and about to contribute to a housing project through his local church.

Making a huge leap in your career is not straightforward. This is particularly true if this involves a change of field (for example, moving from marketing to photography) or a major change of lifestyle (for example, from financial director to author). It's a risky process because it's about moving from known to unknown. However the risk will often be magnified by those who gleefully tell us 'I know someone who tried that ... they're broke now'. It's easy to turn these exploratory thoughts into a game of 'win or bust'. If you play by those rules, you either risk everything or do nothing.

The idea that we can change careers by gradual and experimental steps can be helpful for many, particularly because this career change can involve juggling a huge number of variables. One huge leap can be one leap too many. Most people in fact move forward more effectively through baby steps, mini-rehearsals, trying on a number of roles to see if they fit. There are many examples of people who have gradually built new careers on this basis – by flexing the job they are in, taking on new roles in the **experimental zone** of work, and using their leisure time to experiment with learning prospects or business ideas.

Hermina Ibarra's excellent book *Career Identities* (Harvard Business Books, 2003) explores the idea of experimentally 'trying on' career roles. Stuart McIntosh, Managing Consultant with Career Management Consultants, takes a slightly different view. He believes that while many people talk about making a huge career transformation, few actually do it. He argues that a gradual change model is more realistic, even though many are trying to discover 'how to turn a pipe dream into a pipeline of potential opportunities', and interestingly he believes that the best time to think about making a change in career direction is while employed, as the pressures of being unemployed can lead to a pragmatic if short-sighted decision to move back into a familiar role and occupation: 'Consider career change more as a process involving bite-sized chunks of activity – explore options by talking to those currently working in these roles. Try it out in your spare time – does it feel right? If not, try something else. If you find an occupation which you are increasingly drawn to, obtain qualifications, experiment, establish credibility by networking within your chosen field: obtain "content" for your new CV and when the time is right jump in the shallow end.'

What will work best for you: the model of out and out experimentation or cautious progress? This will largely be a question of how you feel about risk, and how much of a hurry you're in to make a change. Try not to rule out either too soon. Talk to people who have succeeded using each strategy, and work out what approach will suit you best. However, it's also important to remember that some people make the most important life changes by making far riskier moves than the average: sometimes jumping into the deep end or into completely unfamiliar territory has life-enhancing effects.

Retraining: barrier or gateway?

Even though most people believe that money is not their primary motivator (see **Chapter 4**), it is seen as the main block preventing a move into a new career. In surveys most people over-estimate the cost of retraining.

In practice, there are many different options for retraining, many of them extremely low cost. Instead of doing a full-blown MBA, for example, you can often follow short courses in particular subjects, but at the same level. There are many options for online or distance learning. Your bookshop or local library has a huge amount of learning resources available in book form. If you find it tedious absorbing information from long books, there are many publications now that encapsulate information in brief, giving you bullet-point summaries of everything from management theory to website design. The world is awash with free learning opportunities.

Another option, of course, is to negotiate learning opportunities at work – either in your present job or your next one. Consider learning as part of your benefits package; negotiate both learning and training experiences (which can range from sponsored study to training events, and can also include broadening your range of work experiences). Make sure that you get your employer to be as specific about the learning benefits of the job (for example, committing them to paper after an appraisal) as you would be if they were financial benefits.

'MUST DO' LIST

☑ How far has your plan to date been focused on career progression rather than career enhancement?

☑ How can you begin to explore some of the wider choices that will shape your longer term career?

☑ What training or learning opportunities can you negotiate or create for yourself?

☑ Talk to others about the 'What if' possibilities for your career? What experimental next steps can you take?

☑ What changes are you going to make to your work/ life balance so you don't keep making yourself unfulfilled promises?

Protecting Your Side of the Deal

This chapter helps you to:

❚ Overcome internal barriers to asking for a pay increase

❚ Work out a 'deal' even in voluntary work

❚ Understand how to work out what you're worth

❚ Negotiate the right pay level

❚ Know when to ask for other parts of the deal

That which we obtain too easily, we esteem too lightly. It is dearness only which gives everything its value. Heaven knows how to put a proper price on its goods.

Thomas Paine

WHAT IS THE RIGHT DEAL?

Once you've discovered what a valuable asset you are to your organization and you've moved on from survival mode to a real understanding how you match your employer's preferred outcomes, you may want to look more closely at the deal between yourself and your employer. Is each side clear about what they are getting? Are you getting a good deal?

Is money the only way you are rewarded? It's probably better to start with the word *recognition*. How do you prefer to be recognized for your work? Go back to the list of motivators and career drivers you came up with in **Chapter 4**.

You need to be very clear about what returns you are hoping to get out of work. Some people say that they would happily do the job for half the money, but few mean it. Look at the ways the deal works for you (time, work balance, interesting and challenging tasks, money and other compensations) and also look realistically at areas where you think the deal isn't working. What can be changed? It's important to begin this chapter by emphasizing that for most people something in the deal can be altered by negotiation or role development – but there will, equally, be parts of the deal that can't be altered. Sometimes, for example, employers work to fixed arrangements around working hours, holiday entitlement, or pay. Many employers are, however, becoming increasingly flexible. You can usually negotiate for rather more than you think.

Putting your head over the parapet

When it comes to pay negotiations, most of us wish we didn't have to be in the room. We see it as a nasty, grubby business, or a situation where all of the power is in someone else's hands. Which means, sadly, that we fail to do for ourselves what the organization requires us to do every day: negotiate a fair deal. The difficulty is not negotiation as a skill in itself, but the fact that you are negotiating about *you*. Even seasoned sales or purchasing people find it hard to present a case for themselves.

What goes wrong? It seems to me that we are bad at doing two things: accepting praise and seeking reward. They are closely linked. If employment is about a psychological contract between employer and employee, the reason you are in work is essentially to fulfil a deal. You provide your energy, your expertise, and your time, and the employer receives a tangible contribution to Key Result Areas (see **Chapter 5**).

Too many people avoid asking for the right pay level because they're worried about being seen as an irritant. Be very clear about whether you feel underpaid or under-valued. If you feel you are underpaid in relation to your peers or in relation to what you add to the organization, then you may have a case. If you *know* that you're underpaid compared to other people doing the same job, this will have a long-term demotivating effect (see **Chapter 4**). Often the most difficult judgement call you have to make is to decide how far you are prepared to push for a change in your terms and conditions. On the other hand, how do you feel if nothing changes – and what does this do to your work performance?

If you feel underpaid, or seriously underpaid, this is a niggle that just won't go away. Every pay day presses your buttons. Are you putting more energy into worrying about your pay level than you are into the job?

The power (and weakness) of money

As we saw in **Chapter 4**, money is the easiest motivator to talk about, is often seen as the primary career driver, but often has the weakest long-term effect. That doesn't, of course, mean that you shouldn't be paid what you deserve. In fact, working at a lower pay level than you are worth may be a cause for demotivation.

Many of us struggle with the idea of money. If you feel underpaid, the next section is for you. But remember that feeling underpaid isn't a matter of greed. There are plenty of reasons why you might want to negotiate a raise:

▌ You are working above your level of responsibility, and have done so for some time unrewarded.

▌ Your ideas and your contribution are not valued because of your pay grade.

▌ Others do the same job as you and are paid more, even though their results are no better than yours (or possibly poorer!).

▌ You know what contribution you make to the bottom line of your organization, and you feel you are not compensated accordingly.

▌ You know how much it would cost to replace you!

However, many people feel a great deal of discomfort talking about money at all. This can be for a variety of reasons outlined in **Table 9.1**.

Table 9.1 Reasons for not talking about money, and what happens as a result

I don't want to be seen as grabbing	Are you expected to negotiate a fair deal on behalf of your employer? If you can't do this for yourself, what does it say about your skill set? It's only grabbing if you take more than you deserve. Negotiating a fair settlement is a different matter.
Talking about money is grubby	The feeling of grubbiness passes quickly. Actually, most employers expect you to discuss financial matters openly and objectively.
I'm happy with the going rate	Fine, but do you know what the going rate is? Or are you merely accepting your employer's guesswork?
I don't have the confidence to fight my corner	This is a major block for a lot of people. Some tips: imagine you are doing it for somebody else. Research carefully, so you're presenting facts, not hunches. Offer opportunities rather than demands. Don't wind yourself up to the point where you will take questions or rejection personally. A well thought-out written proposal may be your answer.
I can live on what I earn	Fine, if it's true, and you're happy to leave it at that. There are plenty of employers who rely on this level of employee passivity. However, if you feel you are underpaid compared to your colleagues or peers, this will reduce your motivation and performance.

If I ask for a pay rise and don't get it, I'll feel forced to move on to a new job	Who invents these rules? This is negotiation by ultimatum: consent, or I go. Even if you win, holding a gun to your employer's head is disastrous for long-term relationships. Look for win/win, not killer moves.
Work is about more than money	True, at least in terms of the motivation of most people. But your salary is about more than your ego: it's what your labour buys in terms of time, leisure, accommodation, lifestyle, or family commitments. You add value to your work so you can add value to other parts of your life. If you are a high earner, put money back into the economy by providing work for others, and step up your charitable contributions.
I am uncomfortable earning a high salary when other people work harder than me and earn less	Sadly, pay levels are not related to the quantity of work you do, and sometimes not always related to quality. There is a premium paid for scarcity and complexity, but there is usually some connection between what you are paid and the value you add, or save. This may be in straight £££s, or sometimes in profile – a hospital administrator may be paid more than a nurse because of avoiding PR nightmares rather than skill level.
Higher pay means bigger headaches	Possible, but not automatic. Look at the number of people who get promoted simply to keep them out of trouble!

VOLUNTARY WORK OR LOW-PAID PROJECTS

There are times in life when we offer our work for nothing. In fact, society wouldn't function without the voluntary contributions of time and effort which go into parent–teacher associations, scouts and guides, church groups, community projects, prison visitors and so on.

The attractive thing about voluntary work is that it clearly makes a contribution to society or to your local community. Also, it can provide a great opportunity to build up your skills. Handled well, voluntary work contributes to your career. You may pick up transferable skills which lead to paid work, or you may discover learning opportunities.

Sometimes the line between paid and unpaid work can become blurred. Consider, for example, the following three examples of unpaid employment:

I An volunteer company adviser whose advice is not taken as seriously as a less qualified but salaried manager.

I A charity administrator who is not given support or training.

I A training consultant who is offering free sessions, but cannot get the client company managers to commit to a date.

The problem in many cases is, essentially, this: *people value what they pay for*. Or, if money isn't involved, it's still true that people tend to place more value on something that comes at some level of cost, difficulty, or transaction.

It's a reasonably good strategy to offer unpaid or low-cost work when you are starting up your own business, or if you are seeking work experience to bolster your CV. When you do this, remember to look for a 'deal' nonetheless. You might, for example, offer to provide your expertise over a fixed period of time at no charge, but make sure that you ask in return for tangible commitment, for example:

I travelling and other expenses

I access to key people in the organization

▌ the opportunity to attend key meetings

▌ a positive reference, again at the end of the project

▌ honest and accurate feedback at the end of the project.

The last point is crucial. Having undertaken one project you can honestly talk to future organizations about 'what I normally do...', and you can point to at least one past success. If the position is entirely voluntary, the deal should include learning opportunities and resources, as well as real feedback.

Failing to convince your employer or client to give you anything back for your time will make it much more likely that your contribution will be taken far less seriously, and you may find your voluntary contribution rather unfulfilling.

STRATEGIES FOR PROTECTING YOUR SIDE OF THE DEAL

When planning your approach, think through the 10 strategies below. Research your background material carefully, and decide which combination of strategies you are going to use, before referring to the **10-Step Negotiation Checklist** which follows.

Strategy 1: Identifying your true pay range

In paid employment you'll find it helpful to work out what the right 'deal' is between you and your employer. It is a reality that sometimes people find it hard to break through a particular pay barrier. The odd thing is that this is as much to do with psychology as economics. Put in the crudest form, the following statement seems to be true: if you feel you are worth £20,000 a year, you will earn £20,000 a year. This self-imposed picture will actively limit your options. The opposite – believing you are worth £100,000 and so automatically getting it – isn't so straightforward – you can't just pick a figure out the air. However, what you can do is to conduct a personal pay review:

▮ What is your job worth, on average, on the open market? What are the upper and lower points of the pay scale for your job?

▮ What salary would your employer have to pay to replace you?

▮ What factors prompt an employer to pay above-average rates of pay?

▮ What would you have to offer to secure a pay in the top 10% pay band for your occupation and sector?

If your job is rarely advertised on the open market, how do you know what it's worth? It's surprising how many employers pick a salary level out of the air when advertising a new position. And the reality is that, in terms of responsibility, know-how, and experience, there really is very little difference between a £40,000 job and a £50,000 job, and even less difference between a £50,000 job and a £75,000 job. It's a question of employer and market expectations, and a certain amount of guessing on behalf of recruiters.

Negotiating pay is like any form of negotiation; you need to begin from a position of knowledge. How do you find out the pay range for your occupation? Here are some suggestions:

▮ Advertised vacancies: scrutinize the stated requirements.

▮ Search online job boards by sector and region.

▮ Keep active links with professional institutes or other bodies where fellow professionals gather.

▮ Refer to data published by the salary surveys (e.g. IDS or The Reward Group), or surveys published by trade magazines, or free online data published by the Office for National Statistics.

▮ Network with recruitment consultants: they can often give you good feedback on market factors and pay rates.

If you ever want to find out what a job pays, you will rarely be successful if you ask directly. Better, for example, to get a broad feeling for the market rate, add 10%, and then approach a recruitment consultant or employer and say 'I understand that a job at this level pays around £xxxx – is that about right? Whether you get confirming noises or a sharp intake of breath will tell you a great deal.

When job-seeking you should only negotiate pay when the employer has decided they can't live without you. Similarly the best time to renegotiate your salary, is when your employer is most aware of your 'offer', most aware of the value you bring to an organization.

Strategy 2: Find the right decision-maker

Is the correct decision-maker your immediate boss or someone else? Who makes the final decision? Are there any external constraints like company policy (for example, pay rises are only given at certain times of year). If so, ask around to identify exceptions to the rule – you can usually find them.

If your boss is the decision-maker, think carefully about the way he or she likes to handle information, questions, and new suggestions. Some managers are very happy to respond on the spot, others need some thinking and reflection time. If you have a reflective person, it might be a good idea to flag up what you want to talk about in advance, and possibly provide a written summary of the background evidence. Don't state in advance exactly what kind of a figure you are looking for.

It's obviously unwise to begin negotiations on a day when your boss has been carpeted for weak cost control. A good time is when you have just received praise for doing something well. A bad time, obviously, is when your company is under financial strain or has just lost a key client. Don't let the fact that your company is laying off staff put you off asking for a pay rise (or a change of job, for that matter) – very often companies take active steps to retain key staff at times like this.

Strategy 3: Do Your homework on pay levels

Go back to the earlier part of this chapter to identify methods of working out what your job is worth. Don't go into a pay negotiation without:

▌ An upper figure or range – your target zone. Don't try to guess what the job is worth. Find out the upper and lower points of the salary typically paid for this kind of job. Rehearse all the reasons why you should be paid in the top 25% of this band.

▌ A fallback position – what you're prepared to accept.

▌ An alternative fallback position – what you are prepared to offer and accept if no additional money is available. (This is a good time to negotiate conditions which match your main career drivers, see **Chapter 4**.) The advantage of negotiating non-financial factors at this point is that your boss may be relieved to be able to offer you something low on cost and high on imagination.

Strategy 4: Don't confuse a pay rise with a promotion

All too often a discussion about pay turns into a conversation about promotion, and vice versa. Be very clear about the topic of your conversation. A promotion is unlikely to be something you can negotiate as a result of a one-off meeting (although asking for a promotion can be a critical step). The danger is that your objectives become confused – you may end up with a new job title and little else. Worse still, because promotion is a more complicated matter, your request may effectively be put on hold. If you have set out to gain a pay rise, stick to that agenda. If your employer wants to talk about promotion, make that the agenda for a separate meeting.

Strategy 5: Boost your case with hard evidence

Remember, the more your 'pitch' sounds like 'I want more money' the less welcome it will be. Your case should be about job content, responsibility, and about the *future* – how you will continue to contribute. Your boss may not be aware of how your job has changed, and may not be aware of all the projects you are now running. Provide a list of your key responsibilities (before the meeting if this is useful).

Focus carefully on what you are bringing to the deal, remembering to explain in 'win' language which means something to your employer. This is where you can draw upon the evidence you have discovered about the Key Result Areas (KRAs) of your job and organization (see **Chapter 5**).

The points you will emphasize will be:

I tasks you have accomplished that are 'above your pay grade'

I projects you have handled personally

I times when you have rescued victory from the jaws of defeat

I all the times you match KRAs in the job

I the many occasions when you have gone the extra mile.

Chapter 11 will give you some more tips on spotting your achievements. Try not to focus just on the past: describe what you can do in the future.

Strategy 6: Anticipate the other side of the deal

It's fairly likely that an employer will want to look at the other side of the coin. How have you been performing recently? What problems have been experienced? A manager will often want to link the idea of a pay rise to your present and future performance. Again, you need to be on top of the information: have facts and figures ready, if needs be, to justify the claim that you are making a significant contribution. Deal frankly and openly about your success or failure in meeting objectives and targets. Don't be put off by the first attempt to put off a pay conversation until your next appraisal. If it's important enough for you to raise the issue today, it's important enough to be discussed today.

Strategy 7: Treat the conversation as normal

If you sound as if you are asking for something unusual or exceptional, the harder it will be to get a 'yes'. Your boss is more likely to reflect back to you that your request is, indeed, unusual, and outside the scope of what the system allows. The more your tone of voice suggests that this kind of conversation and is perfectly natural, the more your manager is likely to accept the idea that a one-off pay review makes sense.

Strategy 8: Seek 'and also' solutions

It may be that you have to accept a deal cut in a way you didn't expect. Your employer might, for example, ask you to take on additional responsibilities to prove yourself. You may get offered something much lower than your ideal salary. Remember that once the money issues are resolved, there are still other elements in the deal. You may be able to ask for an early review date. You may be able to negotiate a bonus or a better commission structure. You may be able to fix some demotivators – for example, trading in a company car that you find tax inefficient and moving to a car allowance scheme (or vice versa). And don't forget that giving in on the money front gives you even more reason to seek solutions which relate to your non-financial motivators.

If your employer won't move on the money, ask for an early salary review date, or an enhanced bonus, or some other way of improving the package quickly. Be careful you don't give away concessions unnecessarily, for example, accepting a pay rise now but agreeing to skip a pay review next year.

Strategy 9: Don't be coercive

Holding a gun to your employer's head ('I'll have to get my CV updated' or 'I'll be forced to look elsewhere') just doesn't work.

Do that and you have no offer, just a threat. All you do is place a big question mark over your commitment and loyalty. This strategy is perceived as very threatening by employers, and the end result is often that the employee leaves the organization anyway, often for the wrong reasons.

Similarly, it won't work if you try to use an external job offer to force your employer's hand. This, too, sounds as if you have already made your mind up to leave. You might, just, get away with saying 'I'm being pestered by head-hunters who keep offering me jobs, which has prompted me to think carefully about why I enjoy this role. However, I'd like to have a meeting to look at my pay package.' Remember, it's a negotiation, not a stand off.

Strategy 10: Be prepared for a deferred decision

Don't be surprised by a blocking response ('my hands are tied ...') or a delaying response ('I'll have to run this by the MD...'). The result of both approaches is usually that the problem is transferred to someone else. The problem is that the only message that becomes transferred is that 'Amit wants a pay rise', which if you're not present can easily translate into 'Amit's complaining'. Offer to contribute to further discussions in person or in writing so your message can't easily be misinterpreted.

If you find you have to work around a deferred decision, don't give up. If someone else is going to be involved, and the discussion will take place in your absence (e.g. your boss is going to negotiate with HR) do make sure that all the evidence gets included in the discussion. You should, for example, provide your boss with a written summary of all of the hard evidence behind your 'pitch'. If you put your terms in writing, sound as upbeat and reasonable as you can. Offer to go along to the meeting if it's appropriate.

10-STEP NEGOTIATION CHECKLIST

You may not want to try all these techniques on the same occasion. Choose your time carefully, and work out an approach that will be appropriate.

Step 1: Don't back your manager into a corner

Be careful - some managers become very defensive when it comes to pay issues. No matter how carefully you make your case, what they will hear is 'you're not treating me right' or 'I'm unhappy'. **Do** be careful to reinforce your suggestions for change with plenty of positive comments.

Step 2: State your objectives clearly

Whether you're springing a meeting on your boss at an opportune moment or conducting a pre-arranged meeting, **Do** make it very clear what the meeting is about. Try not to be vague by talking about 'prospects' or 'the future'. Make it very clear that you want to talk about your contribution to the organization and you're asking for a pay rise.

Step 3: Make your pitch

Your opening needs to be about your contribution, and not about money. **Don't** make your bid sound like a complaint. Be careful to ensure that you communicate how much you enjoy the job, particularly those parts where you have extended your job content.

Do try something like 'I'm aware how much my job has grown, and how much more I'm contributing to the organization. I'd like to tell you why I believe I deserve a pay rise.'

Step 4: Begin and end with positives

Because it's vital that you don't turn a pay negotiation into a complaints session, it's really important that you begin and end your 'pitch' (see below) on a positive note. Start with a statement like 'first of all I'd like to say how much I've enjoyed the job over the last 12 months'.

Don't make it sound as if there is a huge 'but' coming along. Be clear: 'I'd like to think I have an exciting future here, and that I've got a lot to offer. And that's why I'm asking for a pay rise.' If the meeting ends up without that result, make sure you end positively but with a clear agreement about when the issue is going to be discussed.

Do create the right impression: look, act and sound like a person already holding down a job paying the kind of salary you want. Don't negotiate a pay rise in an old suit.

Step 5: Don't talk about your bottom line
Don't be tempted to talk about what you 'need' financially, or about your financial commitments. Talk about the value you add.

Step 6: Let your boss shoot first
Don't jump in with an amount. Spell out your 'offer' first, and find out what your employer is prepared to put on the table. Even if your employer asks 'What did you have in mind?' It's worth at least one attempt to find out what might be possible: 'Perhaps you could let me know what kind of pay range might be available' and when you have an answer ask: 'what would I need to do to be paid in the top end of that range?'.

Step 7: Don't accept the first offer as final
If your pitch is good, there's no reason why you shouldn't achieve a pay rise. Thousands do every week. **Don't** believe that the first offer, particularly if it's made quickly, is the last word. This is where your background planning is essential. How does the offered pay rise relate to your anticipated range? If you have to come back, reinforce your 'pitch' again and give clear, concrete reasons why your pay offer may not be enough. Think of other ways you can cut the deal (see below).

Step 8: Watch for the brush off
Don't allow your approach to be brushed aside with a throwaway line, for example, when you say 'I'd like a pay rise' your boss might answer 'Who wouldn't?'. It's a commonly used technique. Press on. If you think your boss will react that way, maybe it would be a good idea to set up a meeting with a clear agenda.

Step 9: Negotiate like a professional
Here are a few tried and tested techniques:

I Work out the difference between what you are asking for and what the employer is offering. Let's say you are after a £2,000 a year pay rise, and your employer offers £1,000. Divide it by 50, then say 'We're talking about a difference of £20 a week. We pay more than that in photocopying/coffee/stamps'. (Remember that every £1,000 per year is roughly £20 a week.)

I Relate your proposed total salary in monthly terms to the annual bottom line contribution of the job, for example, 'For £2,000 a month salary costs you're going to achieve at least £90,000 savings (or sales, or profit, or output) next year'.

I Reinforce the idea that your memory and knowledge are huge assets.

I Invite (but very subtly) your employer to think about the opportunity costs of not having you around. You might be saying something like 'We're both aware of the time and trouble it would take to go to the open market to fill this post'.

Step 10: Bang the table, but gently
Do stand up for yourself, but be assertive rather than aggressive. Remember that you are now exercising a toughness that your employer probably expects you to

demonstrate to others, particularly suppliers. You're also using negotiation and problem-solving skills, so by demonstrating your ability to cut a deal you are, in effect, adding to the evidence about why you should be paid more.

OTHER JOB ASPECTS YOU MAY WANT TO NEGOTIATE

So far this chapter has looked largely at the issue of pay. This is, largely, because most people find it difficult to negotiate a pay rise, particularly if their pay rate is considerably lower than it should be. There are, of course, many other things from your wish list you might want to negotiate: flexible working hours, time off, non-cash benefits such as health care, child care, or other elements that you know will help to motivate and retain you, such as learning opportunities or the chance to work on new projects.

In principle, the approach is the same as asking for money, and is touched on above. It's usually a good idea to go into a pay discussion with a secondary list of things you would like to get out of the deal. Alternatively, if the money is right, you can use the negotiation steps listed above to ask for other things (you must, of course, observe sensible limits in terms of how much you ask for in one year!). The basis for negotiation and discussion is the same: remind your employer of your overall contribution to the specific and important needs of the organization, state what you are looking for, and indicate how this will enable you or motivate you to add to your 'offer'.

So, for example, if you would really like to study for a qualification, a good 'pitch' would be to remind your boss of your contribution this year, and to talk about the way your skills have been built up by various learning experiences. Explain why you believe that the right course and a recognized qualification will add value, both to your own work performance and the organization as a whole. Be direct about the costs of the course and any time off you would expect to receive, but then maximize the return on this investment in terms of your improved motivation at a new point on your learning curve (see **Chapter 8**).

Remember that in many ways these add-ons are much softer options than asking for a pay rise – many of them are far easier to provide, and some of them are virtually cost-free to an employer. You may want to have some of these in your kitbag in a pay negotiation, to throw in if you really can't get the financial deal you want. You may also want to decide before you go into a negotiation what, for you, would be the best overall mix of pay, terms, opportunities for growth, and job redefinition – and also have a fallback position as well. Don't expect to get the deal right the first time around – since it's a complex mix of financial and other elements, it may require an organic process of change, and also some time for your employer to come round to what you suggest. Perseverance and time can however achieve some very surprising results.

'MUST DO' LIST

☑ Begin your research now into what your job is worth. Establish in your mind very clearly what your job is worth inside and outside your company.

☑ Set clear upper and lower parameters for what you are prepared to accept in terms of a pay rise.

☑ Plan your approach to your pay negotiation carefully, in terms of preparation, timing, and style of approach.

☑ Keep your bid positive and focused on the future. Rehearse what you will say with a supportive friend.

☑ Plan your fallback positions in advance – including the possibility that nothing works!

Career Traps

This chapter helps you to:

▌ Identify and avoid Career-Limiting Actions

▌ Read and manage your boss

▌ Spot career traps

▌ Rethink appraisals, and gain more from them

The difference between a successful career and a mediocre one sometimes consists of leaving about four or five things a day unsaid.

Anon.

CAREER-LIMITING ACTIONS

As you become more attuned to your organization and ways of steering a successful path through it, you will become more aware of the factors that make you successful. You'll also see that some activities and behaviours have exactly the opposite effect. Some of these can be described as **Career-Limiting Actions** (CLAs – see **Table 10.1**). You might like to look, honestly, to see how many of them have got in the way for you.

TABLE 10.1 Career-Limiting Actions

Tasks	**Don't limit yourself to your job description.** If your aim is to irritate, go ahead ...
People	**Don't be over-competitive.** Being competitive is fine, but climbing over the backs of others to reach your personal goals is widely resented.
	Don't gossip and criticize. It may make you entertaining in coffee breaks, but doesn't position you as someone who can be trusted to bring out the best in others.
	Don't hog the credit. Share it. Make sure your boss know who else is working well. If your boss wants the credit, live with that sometimes.
	Don't fail to delegate. Ideally you should be training up your successor.
Your boss	**Don't fail to observe your boss's style.** Don't just do what your boss wants, but do it in the way he or she wants it done. See **Table 10.2** for more details.
	Don't ignore your boss's goals. As our survey pointed out, working in tune with your boss's goals is a great career plus. Blocking them is the perfect CLA.
	Don't feed your boss's pet hates. Tidy that desk, or pick the phone up after three rings. Work out what really irritates your boss, and stop doing it. It's worth the personal struggle, and allows you to negotiate over things that really matter.
	Don't forget the stuff your boss values. Whether it's telephone numbers or the names of her children.
Processes	**Don't put too much or too little in writing.** Each organization has its own internal rules on memos/emails confirming decisions. Learn what

is acceptable and necessary, and always do it
with a light touch rather than sounding bossy.

Don't fight the bureaucrats. Upsetting those
people who want you to fill in Form H76T by
Wednesday only adds to negative messages
about you. Bite the bullet; fill the form in, and
move on.

Don't hold long and unnecessary meetings.
People love short, focused meetings – and rarely
get them.

Attitudes and
Behaviours
Don't dress like a walking CLA. Dress like the
next grade up, not like someone 2 weeks from
retirement.

Don't say NO to everything. Learn to say no, but
as positively as you can. Don't say no just out of
instinct.

Don't say YES to everything. Over-committing
leads to underperformance, and gives you the
reputation of someone who doesn't deliver.

Don't take your moods to work. Try to maintain
a reasonably consistent, friendly style. Smile. It
helps.

Don't get out of touch with your industry.
Happily admitting you are no longer up to date
and using phrases like 'in my time ....' clearly
marks you as disposable goods.

Don't take criticism or rejection personally.
New ideas get shot down all the time. Learn to
bounce back.

Don't communicate badly. Whether verbally or
in writing. Take care to speak and write
accurately and without glaring errors.

Communicate with your boss sparingly and effectively

The relationship with your boss is critical, so use contact time with your boss economically. Popping in for a 'quick word' too often makes you a distraction, and also reinforces the idea that you cannot work unsupervised. Plan your meetings with your boss carefully. Have an informal verbal agenda ('I'd like to talk to you about three things – have you got a couple of minutes?'). Stick to your agenda, and get out quickly, unless invited to do otherwise.

Try not to go to your boss with problems after a task has been delegated to you. This can look like you're trying to hand the task back. Offer solutions, and check resources and likely snags when the delegation takes place.

Don't double-check every detail with your boss. Work out the things you do need to check, and gradually broaden the tasks where you are able to take the initiative. Keep your boss informed (but not over-informed) by writing a weekly report. Try using the **20/5 principle**: a one-page document that takes you about 20 minutes to write, and your boss 5 minutes to read. The workplace is awash with information – help your boss (and other decision-makers) by learning how to communicate concisely but effectively.

'Make sure your boss knows your achievements', says Julia Robertson, MD of Carlisle Staffing Services. 'Ask your boss "is there anything more I could be doing to do my job better, or to develop myself for the next step on the ladder?" Make your boss accountable for helping you achieve the job you want.'

Career coach Derek Osborn asserts that you can create opportunities for yourself through your manager: 'Volunteer for more responsibilities, write terms of reference for the kind of more responsible job or project that you would like and give it to the boss.'

Reading your boss's style

Things often go wrong in the workplace where people misread each other. This isn't just about getting on, but about interpreting the way people prefer to work. **Exercise 10.1** encourages you to check out your boss's style, and see how aware you are of problems.

EXERCISE 10.1 – WORKING OUT YOUR BOSS'S THINKING STYLE

Circle each word or phrase that best describes your line manager (don't leave this lying around at work!).

Table 10.2   Your boss's thinking style

My manager is most concerned with			
Results	People	Principles	Processes
My manager is most concerned with			
Fine details	Explanations	Activity	The big picture
My manager's decision making style is			
Democratic	Consultative	Delegating	Autocratic
My manager's style of working in a team is			
Chairperson	Ideas person	Facilitator	Encourager
My manager is most concerned with			
Facts	Image	His feelings	My feelings
In a meeting my manager prefers to be the			
Boss	Ideas person	Co-ordinator	Analyst
My manager values in other people			
Detail	Ideas	Teamwork	Innovation
My manager prefers feedback on his or her work			
In private	In a small team	In public	Never
My manager likes new information			
Informally, and on the spot	Informally, but with clear facts and explanations	Informally, but with plenty of notice	Formally in writing

AVOIDING CAREER TRAPS

Most of us are capable of being the authors of our own misfortune through Career-Limiting Actions. However there are also *career traps*. Sometimes these are dead ends, decisions that prevent you moving forward. At other times it's about taking the wrong kind of work or making a misguided decision.

Trap 1: Being flattered into accepting a promotion

You may feel pressurized to apply for an internal position because someone suggests that you would be 'perfect for the job'. You don't want to let down the person who suggests that you apply – particularly if it's somebody you respect. The difficulty with an internal position is that both taking it without reflecting and turning a promotion down could be Career-Limiting Actions.

Don't take a job on these grounds without checking the role out carefully. Make sure it is a good match for you, and a good stepping-stone. If it's not, don't be negative or give the impression you are turning down a great offer. State assertively what you *are* looking for, and you may even encourage your employer to offer you something even better.

Trap 2: Hitting the ceiling

The idea of a glass ceiling is familiar to most of us. It's an invisible barrier above which certain kinds of people cannot progress. Women often feel that they hit a glass ceiling in terms of pay and promotion. However, the glass ceiling principle often seems to apply to other groups, too – non-graduates, for example, or those without particular kinds of experience. To break through this kind of barrier, you need to learn from others who have done it before you. It's a hard enough job anyway, but trying to invent new strategies is harder still.

Where the glass ceiling is set around certain kinds of qualifications or experience, you face the same problem as a job applicant. Seek out or encourage exceptions to the rule book, find examples of people who have found a way around the obstacle facing you. Challenge the dominant mindset. If your employer sets a requirement you cannot meet, ask *why* the restriction exists, and show how you are a good match in other ways. If you're told that only graduates get to a certain pay grade, show how your training and the projects you have undertaken are equivalent to a degree. Few glass ceilings have a rational basis to them – it's mostly about continuing 'the way we do things here'.

Trap 3: Becoming overspecialized

Specialist expertise is valued by organizations, but not necessarily in senior staff. It's a difficult balancing act. The job will often require you to acquire fairly specialized know-how and skills, but it's often best to adopt these on a project-by-project basis and move on each time to new challenges. Specialist knowledge is of course the key if you intend to develop a portfolio or consultancy career. In a general management role it's seems unwise to be overspecialized – although it's unclear whether companies fail to promote those whose experience is too narrow, or simply because organizations don't believe that specialists look the part.

Those with overspecialized profiles (e.g. in IT or accountancy) sometimes find it hard to step into the very top jobs. The key issue is of course not just what's on your CV, but how you are perceived by the organization.

For many in our survey in **Chapter 2** a generalist role was the key to success, for example Mike Wallwork: 'Providing you have strong communication and leadership skills a little knowledge of a lot of subject goes further than in-depth knowledge of a narrow business base in terms of career progression.'

It's also possible to get pigeon-holed if you're stereotyped. This
may, ironically, be because of a past action. You succeeded in
getting noticed – and you've been seen in the same light ever
since. The only way out of this is challenge assumptions: 'I
expect you think I'm mainly interested in research. Actually,
I've really enjoyed some of the training I've been doing
recently ....'

Trap 4: Getting into a rut

A career rut is a state of inertia. You recognize the symptoms
when you are in one: you have probably stopped learning,
your job offers few challenges, and your motivation to undertake tasks you have done before decreases every month. Why
don't you get out of the rut? Because it's a *velvet rut* – and it's
just a little too comfortable to get out of. The money's good,
you have an easy journey to work, and the grass is always
greener ....

Being in a rut can be a career trap because we start to lose
awareness of our lack of energy and contribution. In a way, we
become a little too relaxed about our performance. We start to
take pride in the fact that we don't need to learn new-fangled
ideas or techniques. We begin to lose touch with what's going
on in our company and outside it in our industry.

There's only one way out of this trap. Adapt your rut into
something different, or focus on the real reasons why you want
to change.

Trap 5: Accepting the poisoned chalice

Sometimes the position you've been flattered into accepting
turns out to be full of problems. If your career hasn't been
actively sabotaged, you certainly feel as you've been set up to
fail from the outset. Learn to spot the warning signs, some of
which are set out below:

I Change is necessary, but the person who institutes it is unlikely to survive in the job. Check this one out by finding out why change is necessary and who has a vested interest in opposing it.

I The job is unwinnable: objectives are confused or conflicting.

I The job is seriously under-resourced in terms of staff, budgets, or both.

I The role reports to two managers or more with conflicting styles or objectives.

I No-one has lasted in the job for more than 12 months.

I Your role is so ringed around by rules, restrictions or bureaucracy that you'll be swamped with paperwork from day one.

I People affected by the job have vested interests and want to preserve the *status quo*.

I Your new boss hates people who seem more talented or successful than him.

I The job can't be done by someone who also needs to sleep and have any kind of relationships outside work.

Trap 6: Taking on a challenge without the resources to succeed

One of the biggest career traps happens when you take on a role that has demanding targets but does not have the matching level of resources to allow you to succeed. Worse still, you may have a line manager who is not only convinced you will fail, but is unconsciously making sure that you do.

This has been called the 'set-up-to-fail syndrome', where managers move into a vicious circle which ends up undermining underperformers. Authors Manzoni and Barsoux suggest that what happens is that managers start to unconsciously undermine the performance of the staff who report to them through ineffective feedback and weak interventions, or sometimes by actively putting them in situations where failure is inevitable. The result is a downward cycle of negative perception:

> The subordinate sees the boss as intransigent, interfering, and hypercritical; the boss sees the subordinate as inept, uncooperative, and indecisive. They are well and truly caught up in the set-up-to-fail syndrome.
>
> *The Set Up To Fail Syndrome* (Harvard Business School Press 2002)

A very simple example is where a manager constantly delegates to your weaknesses (so you continue to underperform) rather than to your strengths.

It's easy to get into the beginning of a cycle which ends up with a negative appraisal and a reputation that you have been promoted beyond your competence. There is a solution: be clear before you take on a job what problems need to be solved, be aware of your strengths, and encourage your employer to offer you projects that match your strengths.

Trap 7: Failing to manage others

You can also fall into career trap by being seen as a poor manager of other staff. This, again, is a matter of perception rather than reality. Your superiors probably won't have first-hand experience of your style as a manager or supervisor, but they *will* judge you by the results of your team, and by the number of problems that are generated along the way. A fairly clear sign of difficulties is where you experience above-average staff retention problems, or your staff regularly complain about you to other managers.

Be aware that the performance of your subordinates reflects on you, and also that a good, productive relationship with your team may be taken as a benchmark for progress. Or, in other terms: 'be careful how you treat people on your way up ...'.

There are endless books written on management, but one principle stands out: whatever your management style, whether tyrant or guru, be consistent. Nothing disturbs staff like having to second guess which way up you're going to be in the morning.

HOW OTHERS CAN HELP PULL YOU OUT OF A CAREER TRAP

Sometimes you're only way out of a trap is for someone to throw you a lifeline. This means that it's vital to manage supportive relationships.

Finding out how others see you, whether they are decision-makers or not, is vitally important. Sometimes you pick this up from passing comments, but it's helpful to know as much as you can. Trusted colleagues will give you a straight answer to the question: 'What does X think of me?', but sometimes it's easier to ask about the task rather than about you: 'Why was that helpful? How could I have done a better job?'.

'Broaden your horizons within the organization' is a theme of many responses to our survey in **Chapter 2**. This is about networking formally or informally. On the formal level you may offer to be part of a project or task team. Informally, you may find an opportunity to have lunch or coffee with members of other departments. You may also rub up against them working on charitable projects.

You may also find it useful to talk to people outside your organization: consultants, suppliers, sister or parent companies, for example. An outside perspective often helps.

The message is clearly this: when reshaping your career, keep your eyes and ears open; not only in work but outside work, because sometimes opportunities come in surprising circumstances. You'll also find it helpful to manage relationships around you at work, particularly with your boss.

RETHINKING APPRAISALS

How useful was your last appraisal as a career development conversation? Many dislike appraisals and find them stressful, unproductive, or both. Interestingly, many managers would also like to avoid appraisals. As a management tool, appraisal has many limitations. If it's used as a way of correcting behaviour or offering praise, it tends to be ineffective because of the long gap between meetings. Efficient managers know that most problems need fixing immediately, and the best way to offer praise is usually on the spot.

First of all, plan how you're going to deal with negative feedback, try to concentrate on the observable behaviours that your boss wants to see, and the outcomes that need to be achieved. Don't let your personality get in the way, and don't blame others or 'the system' for your mistakes. South African career specialist Andrew Bramley suggests that the real key is 'getting your ego out of the way when things don't go your way, solving problems without blaming everyone in your path'.

Start with a quick check on what was agreed at your last appraisal. Think these through carefully before you start. If you begin a meeting by apologizing for the things you committed to last year but have failed to deliver, the meeting is going downhill from the start.

Recruiter Linda Walmsley says: 'If there is an appraisal scheme make the most of it. Get your manager to note your strengths and make sure that you take advantage of any development opportunities that are offered. This could be a specific training course or something as simple as being more self-aware.'

The way that your manager *feels* at the end of the process is as important as the facts and details written down on the appraisal record.

Turning an appraisal into a career conversation

Some organizations offer meetings which are specifically focused on career development, but many try to incorporate this theme into an appraisal. There may be times when you want to do this as well.

First, ask for a meeting to look at your career development, and make sure that isn't seen as a euphemism for a request for a pay rise or promotion. You are in fact trying to find an opportunity to use the four-stage **SIGN** method outlined in **Figure 10.1.**

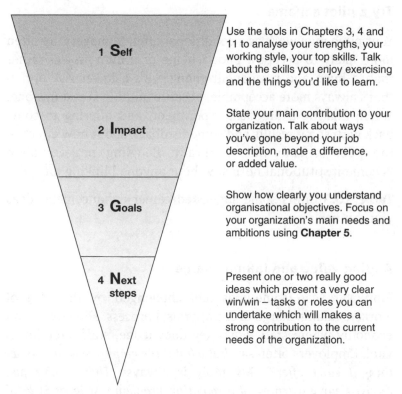

1 **S**elf	Use the tools in Chapters 3, 4 and 11 to analyse your strengths, your working style, your top skills. Talk about the skills you enjoy exercising and the things you'd like to learn.
2 **I**mpact	State your main contribution to your organization. Talk about ways you've gone beyond your job description, made a difference, or added value.
3 **G**oals	Show how clearly you understand organisational objectives. Focus on your organization's main needs and ambitions using **Chapter 5**.
4 **N**ext steps	Present one or two really good ideas which present a very clear win/win – tasks or roles you can undertake which will makes a strong contribution to the current needs of the organization.

Figure 10.1   The SIGN method for offering a win/win at appraisal

Well-conducted appraisals are part of the retention process; your company is asking 'how can we build and retain our best people?'. Turned into a career conversation, you can move away from complaints to positive statements: *'Here is an opportunity I have identified that draws on my top skills ... I will benefit from doing it because/You will benefit if I do this because ... .'* In this kind of language it's much more difficult for an employer to say no. However, do think carefully about your boss's negotiating style. How will your boss react to your wishlist, your analysis of the organization's needs, and your requests?

Try a pilot scheme

Your pitch may work as a conditional offer. Managers are often more likely to accept a pilot scheme or a mini-project rather than a huge and permanent change. It's a lower risk option that's always more acceptable, because nothing is cast in stone. You're floating a practical experiment, and offering to come back with some results and some feedback about how effective the pilot scheme was. Naturally, fledgling projects often become institutional norms without anyone blinking an eye.

Table 10.3 offers some suggested career enhancement ideas you can use.

Adding value and taking charge

Employers can sometimes feel challenged by the idea of workers taking charge of the appraisal process. However, in an economy where staff retain key knowledge, staff retention is vital. Employers often say *'but what if the employee wants something I can't offer?'*. My reply is always: *'Then you've just received early warning of a retention problem.'* At least 50% of the time it makes good economic sense to redesign the job of a key player rather than lose him or her to a competitor – an idea to keep up your sleeve when negotiating your future!

Table 10.3 Career enhancement ideas

▮ What skills and know-how do I want to acquire in the future?

▮ Which teams or individuals would I like to work with?

▮ Which projects or clients would be perfect for me?

▮ Which of my career drivers are not being fully addressed?

▮ What will motivate me even more?

▮ How might I be able to reduce or delegate tasks I find demotivating?

▮ What should my employer be doing to retain me?

▮ What specific projects or areas of responsibility can I suggest to improve my job?

▮ What project ideas, initiatives, or pilot studies can I suggest?

▮ How can I communicate the benefits to my employer?

▮ Who else do I need to convince?

▮ What quick wins can I offer my employer that will benefit our customers and bottom line? (See also **Chapter 12** on making your mark in a new job.)

You should be encouraged to come to a meeting at least every 6 months with at least three suggestions of ways you could work more effectively and create new opportunities for the company. Use the SIGN method to structure your conversation. If your boss hasn't asked for this kind of discussion, then suggest it. If your boss is the kind of person who likes to be in control of information, it might be a good idea to mention your key points in advance of the meeting, possibly in writing.

'MUST DO' LIST

☑ Do your homework: show that you fully understand your job, the organization's KRA's, and provide evidence of your individual contribution.

☑ Develop your relationship with your boss carefully: this person has the greatest power to assist or block your future.

☑ Look at the way others have fallen into career traps or committed Career-Limiting Actions. Learn from their mistakes, and find out how they emerged from the other side.

☑ If you're already in a career trap (particularly if it's a velvet rut) take action to move on.

☑ Next time you have an appraisal, see how far you can rethink the process. Use the SIGN method to turn a dull appraisal meeting into an exciting career development conversation that assists you *and* the organization.

Jumping Ship

This chapter helps you to:

▌ Spot when it's time to move on to a new job

▌ Prepare yourself for career transition

▌ Prepare your responses to the tough questions

▌ Identify your motivated skills

▌ Develop your networking skills

▌ Spot your natural team role

The more I want to get something done, the less I call it work.

Richard Bach

MOVING ON

Time to quit?

There's an art to knowing when it's time to move on. All of my clients who tell me they are interested in job change have to face one question: 'What can you do to fix the job you're in?'. This has a double effect. First, people start to take control by beginning some career-related thinking, and feel that they now have more choices. Secondly, it often helps people feel better because they start to value themselves and what they have to offer. For others there is an understandable degree of guilt at feeling that you are betraying an organization that has been home to you for a number of years. The question, however, is still the same: try to look at the possibility of renegotiating your job before you leave.

There are different reasons why you might be thinking about jumping ship. You may be clear that you need a change and confident about throwing yourself on the market. You may have no choice in the matter because redundancy is looming. More probably, if you've go this far in the book, you may feel dissatisfied in your present situation and unsure whether you should move on to a new job or stay and try to fix the problem.

Recruitment training specialist Janet Basford suggest there is a key question you should ask yourself: 'can my existing organization offer me the next stage in my career? If yes, you need to discuss your aspirations with your company and identify how you could move to the next stage. If not, a plan then needs to be prepared looking at a goal and the strategy to bring that goal to life.' Go back to **Chapters 5** and **6** to explore further what you can do to develop a new niche for you with your present employer.

Knowing whether it's really time to move on to a new job isn't easy. If the job is really getting you down, it's tempting to jump at anything. In fact, that's a mistake too many make. On the other hand, staying on too long can be a Career-Limiting Action (see **Chapter 10**), as well as grinding you down.

The first place to begin is to try to get an objective picture of what is going on. Talk confidentially to colleagues and friends who can help you work out the difference between the things you have no control over, and the things you can do something about. Then get some help in the form of a career review. It's important at a time like this to focus on what is going right as well as what's going wrong. Remind yourself – with help from others – of what you've achieved, and what you bring to the role and the organization.

Push and pull

If you decide to move because you can't do enough in the job you're in, be aware of **push** and **pull**. If you're thinking about moving on, there is a powerful force pushing you away from your present job. You may be thinking that you will do anything to find a new boss, a new culture, a new job. However, your new role also exerts a force, but this time it's a force of attraction.

In simple terms, you should only move on when the **pull** of the new opportunity or position is more powerful than the **push** that is propelling you away from the job you are in now. In other words, move on for the right reasons. In fact, if we only respond to the push factor, there are all kinds of dangers. First, you only talk about your reasons for leaving at interview or to recruitment consultants. Secondly, you're not really thinking about your next role. You may even repeat the same mistakes in the next job. Focusing on the **pull** of the new opportunity means that you have to concentrate on what is good about the next job match – good for you, and good for the new organization.

When is the right time to move?

If you feel propelled to change jobs, think about the timing.

You need to have an awareness of the impact of this decision on your CV and on future decision-makers. You may have to face difficult questions in the future about why you moved on from one or more jobs rather too quickly. The issue is about knowing what others consider to be slow, average, and rapid transitions. Industry sectors vary enormously and at different times. Sometimes it's not only acceptable but impressive to move on every 12 months. In some sectors this communicates job insecurity. Ask colleagues and recruiters to give you a sense of the norm. How will this stage of your CV be interpreted now, and in 5 years' time?

BEFORE YOU JUMP

The rule here is simple: don't jump ship without stocking your lifeboat.

Your lifeboat contains your toolkit for a new career: your self-awareness, your skills catalogue, your career drivers, your understanding of the way your personality fits into work, your clear offer to a new employer. Taking time to stock your lifeboat matters whether you're desperate to move on, or reluctant to move from your present company. Without thinking ahead, you don't have a clear message about why you want to change jobs. What will you do if you employer makes you some kind of counter-offer? In other words, how powerful is your impulse to change jobs, and how far have you rehearsed the real reasons for doing so? Getting your overall message right is critical.

Relationship maintenance

It's worth thinking now how you propose to maintain relationships with your present employer. Consider carefully how you handle the exit interview if there is one. Constructive criticism may be helpful, a personal attack on your boss won't. Don't see the last few days in the organization as your chance for revenge or justice; how you leave will be remembered for many years to come, and may affect your future prospects. Say things that will be helpful to improve performance in the workplace, but otherwise a degree of reticence about difficult or failed relationships is best.

Some organizations actively plan to re-hire some staff who leave. Don't discard the idea that this might include you, or that your present employer may become a future customer, supplier, or provider of freelance work.

Answering the killer question

As soon as you feel it's time to move on you'll be interrogated by friends and family, and quickly afterwards by recruiters and employers. The killer question at this stage is 'Why?' Be prepared: you will be asked it very soon. What you answer to 'Why do you want to move on?' will have a powerful effect on your ability to do so.

If you dislike your present situation, the risk is that your only message to recruiters is 'I hate my job'. Watch out for knee-jerk reactions if this is true. You will have very little positive to say about yourself or your last job if you have just resigned in haste. This is one reason why it is probably easier to get a job while you still have one, rather than resign and start looking. It's nothing to do with the mechanics of job search, but it all comes down to your overall message.

Successful career changers know that they have to think in advance about the big questions and rehearse good answers. These are short, clear, and positive answers to key questions such as those outlined in **Table 11.1**. The emphasis is on short (each response should be about 30 seconds) and positive – don't leave any lingering problems or doubts in the questioner's mind. The useful thing about these questions is that they also help you focus on whether you really want to move job. For more questions and answers see *Job Interviews: Top Answers To Tough Questions*.

Who to talk to

Don't try to stock your lifeboat unassisted. Recruit others to help you discover your strengths and plan the next steps of your journey. Check around you for allies. Possibilities will include:

▌ People in the organization who feel the same way you do.

▌ People who have recently left the organization.

▌ A mentor inside your organization whose advice is confidential.

▌ External consultants/clients/ex-colleagues who can keep a confidence.

Table 11.1   Prepared responses to key career transition questions

---

1. Why are you on the market?
Why do you want to move on? Your response needs to be a
balanced mix of positive comments about your present role
and concrete reasons for wanting new opportunities.

2. How committed are you to change?
How strong is your motivation to change jobs? How will you
feel when you have to write your resignation letter? How will
you respond to a counter-offer from your present employer?

3. What do you have to offer?
A brief summary of who you are, what you do, and what skills
and experience you have. You must be able to respond to the
question `tell me about yourself' at any time.

4. What's your track record?
How can you sum up your career, in a nutshell, and make it
sound both interesting and coherent? How will an employer
make sense of your various career decisions?

5. What have you achieved?
Employers buy attitude as well as experience, so wrap the two
up together – make your success stories communicate both
your skills and your attitude to work.

6. What's your working style?
Be prepared to talk briefly and positively about the way you
work, with colleagues, in teams, and with your boss. Be
prepared to talk about the way you manage, and are managed,
and how you operate under pressure.

7. Why you?
The reasons why an employer should choose you over other,
equally qualified candidates.

Don't get carried away by job search until you know where you
want to go, and why. Search for information in a way which
does not become a Career-Limiting Action (see **Chapter 10**).
It's usually possible to find out a great deal from various sources
without clearly flagging up the fact that you are nearly ready

to jump ship. The principle here is to gather enough information before you commit to a decision which could affect the next 10 years of your life. It's exploration in two dimensions: about *you* (what you have to offer, how you work best, the kind of work you feel called to do) and about *what's out there*.

Talk to people in real jobs

Networking is an essential skill when it comes to unlocking the question of what is available to you. We all know that, and yet most of us frantically search around for reasons not to network. It all seems a little too much like either self-promotion or begging.

'I see networking as the biggest single influencing factor whether someone is keen to get promotion within the same company or to move out,' says career coach Claire Coldwell. 'It's about knowing what you have to offer and making sure that others are aware of it, too, so that when opportunities come up, you've already paved the way for a conversation. Apart from which, networking keeps you informed about what's going on and therefore keeps you interested, even at times when you may not be able to see the next move.'

Ten rules of successful networking

1. **Don't call it networking.** Come up with a description that works for you, e.g. 'Fact finding', 'Broadening my horizons', 'Sounding people out'. When you have a term you're happy with, tell people what you're doing.

2. **Think research, not job search.** Your questions should be about information and ideas, not 'are there any vacancies in your firm?'

3. **Step outside your comfort zone, but only just outside it.** No-one can persuade you to change from shrinking violet to networking star of the year. Find a style that works for you rather than not doing anything at all.

4. **Start with people you know.** It helps to begin by staying firmly in your comfort zone. Think carefully about the people you know who themselves know interesting people.

5. **Follow your passions.** Ask about the things that really interest you.

6. **Ask people for something they can deliver.** People generally like to help, so ask them something they can give you. Ask them:

   ▌ How did you get into your line of work?

   ▌ What do you enjoy about it?

   ▌ What's not so great?

   ▌ What's happening in your field of work?

   ▌ What are the competencies of a top performer in your field?

7. **Keep the focus on the person you are talking to, not on you.** Get people to talk about themselves and they will be far more attentive.

8. **When it comes to talking about you ….** make sure you have a clear, brief message and you're prepared responses to key interview questions.

9. **Always seek the bounce-on.** Ask people to introduce you to others who can be equally helpful. Acknowledge the fact that you hate calling people cold, and ask a favour: 'Would you mind telephoning ahead just to say that I will be in touch?'. Try to get three new contacts out of every positive meeting. If your contact runs out of ideas, ask for names of organizations and names of good recruitment consultants.

10. **Remember the fallback question:** 'Who else should I be talking to …?'

HOW TO JOB SEARCH WITHOUT COMMITTING CAREER SUICIDE

A common objection to the networking concept is 'What if my employer discovers that I am seeking another job?' Think about this carefully, as this could be damaging, particularly if you decide to stay where you are in the long run. You half expect a hurt or punitive response. Part of you feels you are 'letting the side down' by looking over the fence. Either way, it's healthy to remember that we're all grown ups, and people change jobs with increasing regularity. Worrying about your employer's response can stop you thinking actively, and leave you only with the strategy of 'taking whatever comes along'. Life might be made difficult for you if it's discovered that you are looking, but don't forget that your boss and the next boss up are also keeping an eye on the marketplace.

The important question is what happens if you do nothing, and the danger of feeling stuck in a rut. Naturally, if your present job is vulnerable, you need to be discreet about investigating alternative jobs. This means that your networking must be focused on people who you can trust. Most recruitment consultants manage this discretion well, but they aren't necessarily the best people to help you discover what's out there – and you do need to know what your choices are inside and outside the company. In addition, don't forget to keep your emphasis on research rather than job search, and avoid saying anything critical about your present employer.

IDENTIFYING YOUR SKILL SET

As soon as you start talking to people you will discover the skills that they use to fulfil the roles they are in. In order to begin preparation for moving on, you need to take stock of your skills – and learn how to communicate them to others. **Chapter 3** touched on this topic, but you can find more detailed advice here.

There are many ways of spotting your skills. **Exercise 11.1** shows you one of them. Most people only have a limited idea of their skills. They tend to talk about the skills that other people have identified in them, or the skills they think they are supposed to have in order to be successful in their line of work.

EXERCISE 11.1 – SKILLS ANALYSIS

1. Divide a piece of A4 paper into three columns as in **Table 11.2**.

2. Go through your work history. Job by job, list all the important activities, situations, problems. What happened as a result of you being in work?

3. Against each identifiable action, write bullet points summarizing the context, what you did (naming the skills you used), and the outcomes you achieved.

Table 11.2   Skills analysis

Context	The skills I used	The outcome

Look at the skills you have identified, and break them down into five in different categories: (1) equipment/machines, (2) people, (3) organizations, (4) information, and (5) ideas.

As you record the results in **Table 11.2** what you are actually doing is composing skill stories. In fact, stories are great ways to communicate your skills. Just as a good story is short, to the point, your skill stories will be clear and concise. A good story has a clear beginning middle and end, and your skill stories will have a clear three-part structure. This helps you to remember your mini-narratives and communicate them in an attention-grabbing way.

The advantage of using skill stories is that you have evidence to back up the claims you make in appraisals or job interviews.

Everyone makes claims – the best performers back them up with evidence, ideally in measurable terms.

Lorraine Reynolds is PA to the MD of a German-owned healthcare company in Cheshire. Before working as a PA she was employed as a holiday rep. It was this mix of language skills and trouble-shooting that secured her a job as a PA within 5 days of returning to the UK. Lorraine used to be apologetic about working abroad but learned how to turn the unusual into the distinctive.

Lorraine's career path has been much assisted, she says, by the ability to communicate her strengths: 'My CV today defines key personal qualities: flexibility, the diplomatic nature of the PA role, my ability to handle sensitive issues.' Lorraine has trained part-time as a life coach which, she says, helps 'equip me to set goals for myself. You learn to focus on the parts of the job that you like, and you're able to work out problems in the job for yourself when you are not getting support.'

THE SKILLS TRIANGLE

The three-part skills story works, essentially, because you are conveying the information that employers find useful and interesting. The three parts of your story in fact fit into the **skills triangle** shown as **Figure 11.1** – a great way of remembering or recording skills.

Begin with a **situation** – a time, place and context where you used a particular skill. It doesn't have to be an earth-shattering event. Even the small stuff picks up your skill set. Next think about your individual **contribution**. What did you do? If your contribution was part of a team, what was your team role, and how effectively did you fulfil it? Finally, don't forget to record

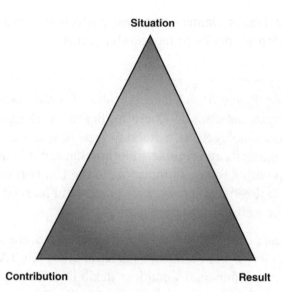

Figure 11.1   The skills triangle

the final outcome – the **result**. Think about what key decision-makers (here, or in another company) consider to be worth-while outcomes.

ACHIEVEMENTS

One of the great spin-offs of skill identification is that you get a change to record and communicate what you have achieved.

Try to express achievements in terms of awards, money, time or percentages if it's possible to do so.

What if you feel you have achieved very little? This could be because you are in a job which is too narrowly focused, but it's far more likely that you have overlooked achievements. Communicating what you have to offer requires you to make *claims*, but to back up claims you need *evidence*. And the best kind of evidence of your *skills* is contained in defined achievements. See **Table 11.3** for more details on pinning down your achievements.

Table 11.3 Prompts to spotting your achievements

1. There will be a problem or a set of obstacles, a challenge. You found some strategy for dealing with the problem – you sought help, or you learned something, or you drew on inner resources.

2. You, personally, did something. If you did it as part of a team, concentrate on what you did personally. There was a result – something changed, something happened.

3. Try asking your colleagues and friends what differences you have made, and what you have added to organizations.

4. Go back through your work diaries and logs. Pick out occasions or projects where you made a difference.

5. Look at your job description. In what ways have you redefined your job? When have you delivered more than expectation?

6. Look at times when you invented new solutions, threw out the rule book, went the extra mile, gave 150%, brought in a key client, etc.

7. Identify moments when you snatched victory from the jaws of failure.

8. Remember to look at achievements in your non-working life. It's often here that you find skills that are undervalued or undeveloped.

9. Spot the times when activities would have failed/lost money/faded away if you had not been there.

10. Record the work activities which give you a sense of excitement and energy.

There are a range of questions that may assist achievement spotting:

- What did I have to do to achieve this?
- What was the task or challenge?
- What did I do personally?
- What was the biggest problem?
- What was my best moment?
- What planning did I need to do?
- What obstacles did I have to overcome?
- How did I work with others?
- What action am I most proud of?
- How did I surprise myself or others?

WHAT IS YOUR NATURAL TEAM ROLE?

There are several other key steps that can build on your skills and achievements and increase your self-awareness. An important area is working out how you operate in a team.

How do you operate in teams? This is an important question in a world where nearly every CV holder claims to be a 'team player'. Identify what you bring to a team. Look at the way you behave most often in teams, that is what roles you fit into most naturally and comfortably. **Exercise 11.2** helps you to identify your natural team role.

EXERCISE 11.2 – DISCOVERING YOUR NATURAL TEAM ROLE

Table 11.4 helps to define the way you naturally fit into a team.

Think about times when you have work in teams. **Read the statements** about each team role.

Give each statement a score of 0, 1, 2, or 3 as indicated.

Table 11.4 Your natural team role

1 Ideas person			
I generally find that in teams or meetings ... **Score:** 0 Hardly ever, 1 Sometimes, 2 Frequently, 3 Most or all of the time			
I frequently come up with new ideas		I enjoy finding new ways of looking at things	
I don't feel constrained by traditional ways of doing things		I can become very absorbed in my own thoughts	
I am relied on to think up solutions		I like to work out difficult problems in my head	
My perspective sometimes surprises people		I like to think 'outside the box'	
Total score			

2 Worker ant			
I generally find that in teams or meetings ... **Score:** 0 Hardly ever, 1 Sometimes, 2 Frequently, 3 Most or all of the time			
I like things to be well planned and structured		I like to see how ideas can be put into practice	
I want to stop talking and start doing		I like to convert talk into action planning	
I am realistic about what will work		I prefer plans to concepts or theories	
I like to have clear goals		I am good at putting plans into practice	
Total score			

3 Progress driver

I generally find that in teams or meetings …

Score:
0 Hardly ever, 1 Sometimes, 2 Frequently, 3 Most or all of the time

I am often assertive or forceful		I am prepared to be unpopular to get results	
I am keen to get through the agenda efficiently and quickly		I am prepared to challenge others	
I tend to influence decisions or outcomes		I am keen to hit goals and targets	
I can be impatient		I am good at negotiating outcomes	

Total score

4 Director

I generally find that in teams or meetings …

Score:
0 Hardly ever, 1 Sometimes, 2 Frequently, 3 Most or all of the time

I take charge of proceedings		I draw other people out and ask for their contribution	
I can get people to agree		I seek a view agreed by the majority	
I can persuade people to accept a decision		I remind the meeting of our objectives	
I see what team members have to offer		I often summarize or clarify what has been said by others	

Total score

5 Explorer			
I generally find that in teams or meetings ...			
Score: 0 Hardly ever, 1 Sometimes, 2 Frequently, 3 Most or all of the time			
I am usually enthusiastic and communicative		I can spot opportunities we can exploit	
I like to make my own contacts outside the group		I am often investigating external resources	
I suggest useful connections and contacts for others		I prefer interesting people who have something to contribute	
I am active and optimistic		I like to draw on outside ideas	
Total score			

6 Analyst			
I generally find that in teams or meetings ...			
Score: 0 Hardly ever, 1 Sometimes, 2 Frequently, 3 Most or all of the time			
I keep calm and can think clearly		I tend to be objective and not caught up in enthusiasm	
I like to check the facts		I am good at organizing the work to be done	
I like to have supporting data		People sometimes think I am too analytical	
I enjoy analysing things		I tend to see all the options available	
Total score			

7 Consultant

I generally find that in teams or meetings …

Score:
0 Hardly ever, 1 Sometimes, 2 Frequently, 3 Most or all of the time

I am called in to deal with particular subjects or problems		I offer skills or knowledge which are in short supply	
I am seen as an expert		I am not interested in things that I cannot make a specific contribution to	
I have specialized knowledge		I want to be useful to several groups rather than a long-term member of one group	
General discussion bores me		I want to pass on my expertise	
Total score			

8 Task master

I generally find that in teams or meetings …

Score:
0 Hardly ever, 1 Sometimes, 2 Frequently, 3 Most or all of the time

I get things done, on deadline		I am concerned that things may go wrong	
I tend to worry about the details		I can be a perfectionist	
I remind people of deadlines		People consider me a safe pair of hands	
I spot errors in documents or plans		I can be relied on to make things happen	
Total score			

9 Team builder			
I generally find that in teams or meetings …			
Score: 0 Hardly ever, 1 Sometimes, 2 Frequently, 3 Most or all of the time			
I like people to get on with each other		I get on with most kinds of people	
I feel that agreement is important		I go with the majority feeling	
I support ideas that are in the common interest		I like to build up relationships between team members	
I want to get to know people better		I encourage teams to meet up socially outside work	
Total score			

Add up your total score for each box and write your top three team roles in **Table 11.5** below. You may find that you have several with the same score. If so, give priority to roles where you operate proficiently *and* comfortably.

Table 11.5   My top three team roles

1.

2.

3.

Figure 11.2 summarizes these team roles under three headings: Action, People, and Thought. You might find it interesting to look back at the primary skills you identified earlier in this chapter and see how many of them fit with the team roles you have listed in **Table 11.5**.

Action-focused roles	Progress driver
	Worker ant
	Task master
People-focused roles	Director
	Team builder
	Explorer
Thought-focused roles	Ideas person
	Analyst
	Consultant

Figure 11.2   Three categories of team roles

How does this help? Firstly, it may give you insights into some of the problems you have experienced in your present role. For example, you may be working in a team which has no natural task master, so projects don't get completed. You may be frustrated at not being able to exercise a leadership role (for example, progress driver or director). You may be a great Ideas Person but this is undervalued by your present employer.

Knowing more about the way you fit into teams can help you to look carefully at your next job. Try to identify the people you will have to work with on a daily basis, and talk to as many of them as you can. Find out which teams are already working well, and which teams aren't. Ask what makes those teams successful, and how they have overcome difficulties in the past. At a job interview you may even ask directly about the contribution you would be expected to bring to a team, and explore this in more detail if you think you won't be playing to your strong suite.

Relation to Belbin types

The team roles described above should relate, roughly, to your 'Belbin type'. The Belbin test is one of the most widely known assessments of team type and performance. For further details see www.belbin.com. To know your Belbin type, take a formal assessment using the Belbin test, and your results should be checked against the way other people see you, particularly work colleagues.

'MUST DO' LIST

☑ Who can you talk to in order to find out when and how to move on?

☑ Record your primary skills. Try communicating skill stories during your next appraisal.

☑ What skills do you perform at a high level? What skills do you enjoy using? How many of these skills are you able to use in your present job?

☑ What have been your biggest achievements during the last 12 months?

☑ Check out your natural team roles. How often do you get a chance to perform in these roles?

The JLA skill cards

Both this book and *How To Get A Job You'll Love* outline a range of techniques for identifying your motivated skills. There is another tool available: the JLA Skill Card Sort – designed to spot your primary skills and show you how to communicate them to decision-makers.

The Skill Cards come with a full set of instructions for use in career development.

See www.johnleescareers.com for further details.

Making Your Mark in a New Job

This chapter helps you to:

▌ Quickly make a strong impression in a new role

▌ Build on your new job from the job offer onwards

▌ Use the critical stages in your new position to assist career development

▌ Spot the minefields

▌ Identify quick wins

I don't know anything of luck. I've never banked on it, and I'm afraid of people who do. Luck to me is something else: hard work and realizing what is opportunity and what isn't.

Lucille Ball

ACCEPTING THE OFFER

It's healthy to take a step back when you accept a new job. Start by looking at the requirements of the role. How far can you negotiate the content of your future job? Sounds unlikely? Think again. You have far more possibility of affecting job content at the point of accepting a job offer than you probably will have at any other time in the first 2 years in employment. This is a time when, for a brief moment, you have some leverage over a number of elements:

I Your **salary** – this should only be negotiated when an employer has come to the firm decision to appoint you.

I Other aspects of your **financial package** – for example, pensions, medical insurance, and so on – whatever is important to you.

I **Job content** – by making your employer a positive 'offer' you will be able to exert some influence, however small, over job content.

I Any **other aspects** – you may be able, for example, to negotiate longer holidays or flexible working arrangements.

These ideas need some unpacking because, at first sight, they may seem either idealistic – or possibly only something that very confident senior candidates can achieve. Not so. As we have seen, any job is a 'deal' between employer and worker – it's just a matter of whether you realize what cards you hold. Trying to negotiate any of these points before the job offer stage is a bad idea, because it can give an employer a reason not to appoint you. Resist the temptation to discuss anything in the package until you hold an offer (with the possible exception of job content, which you can ask about at interview in order to demonstrate your interest). Once an employer has fallen in love with you, you're playing by different rules: a trip has been switched in the employer's mind, and now they're worried that you won't accept. Be aware of the opportunity cost of having to go back to the market and seek new candidates.

However, do be aware that you can't negotiate on everything. Stick to the aspects that matter to you most. In terms of planning your future, the best strategy if the money is acceptable is to focus on the job itself. Be careful – what you don't want to do is sound as if you are complaining and you don't really want the job. Always begin and end any comment on job content with a positive comment, for example: 'Let me begin by saying how exciting this job opportunity is for me. There are just one or two things I need to discuss with you before I accept. The good news is it's not the money! What I'd like to do is to ask you to think about restructuring the role to increase the amount of training I'll be doing. If you remember, at interview we discussed how important this is to me. Now I'd like to suggest two things that will benefit the company.'

A fall-back strategy is to ask for a chance to begin certain activities within a certain time frame 'OK, so how about if I'm given a chance to run my own accounts within 6 months or so?'

If you'd rather run a mile than make any kind of counter-offer before beginning a job, just think what you're throwing away – the chance to shape the job from the outset. Negotiating the job content is both good for you and good for the organization. And it can make the difference between early promotion and career blocks.

Finally, if you're still struggling with the idea, try for one thing. Look at what you think may be the difference between the job on offer and the job you'd really like to do, and ask for one thing to be changed. 'Thanks for the offer. I'm delighted. There's just one thing I'd like you to consider before I accept. I'd like a chance to do more —— in the job. If we can fix that, I'll be on board!' As long as you begin and end your comment on a positive note, you've a high chance that it will happen.

FIRST STEPS TOWARDS CAREER SUCCESS

Unless you have a relative who owns the company, no one starts out at the top.

When new employees join an organization, particularly those at the beginning of their careers, they often assume that a career ladder is best scaled step by step. In other words, you work hard on the present rung of the ladder and someone will give you a shove up to the next level. All you need to do, it seems, is to hang on and do a great job. However, some will discover that it often takes an unconventional route to climb your way to the board room. Those who are successful (in terms ranging from promotion to job satisfaction) come to learn that organizations only play a limited part. Often it's a matter of finding supporters, speaking the right language and reading the runes, combined with a strong focus on the next right step. And, undoubtedly, a strategy for coping with failure and moving on quickly. These people know the difference between things they can change, and the factors which are outside their control.

BEGINNING A NEW JOB

Your first 2 weeks in the job may have far more impact on your career prospects than any other fortnight you spend in the role.

Your first strategy is to listen, learn, and ask intelligent questions. Find out who the key people are in the organization – the people who will make decisions about your future. But first of all start by identifying two kinds of people:

1. People who are visibly doing a good job. These people will eventually be good people to talk to, but for the moment just watch and learn.

2. People who are **information brokers** within the organization – the people who know where things are, who does what, and who to ask questions. Hunt around – these people exist in every organization. Sometimes it's the managing director's PA, sometimes it's the security guard on reception.

Do your homework

You've probably already done a great deal of research in order to get an interview and a job offer. Don't stop just yet. In fact, dig deeper: identifying the major problems and headaches within your organization will give you vital clues about what needs to be done to create success. Look out for company information you can take home and absorb, so you can learn about products, initiatives, supply chain, customer contacts.

Read external literature like the company report and press releases, and internal information, too. Spend time absorbing the language of the organization: how does it express itself? And don't forget to have a good look at organizational charts. Remember the names and job titles of people that matter.

Keep a notebook. Write down names, procedures, contact numbers. Learn the names of key people. Spot the people who can make your job easier, or can make it hell. Try not to step on toes at this stage – first impressions matter, and you don't want to inadvertently make life enemies now. If the stationery department will only issue you a notepad on a Tuesday between 2 and 3pm, run with it. Making waves now could be a serious **Career-Limiting Action** (see **Chapter 10**), because people are making their minds up about you.

Hit the deck running

Work out the key tasks of your job – how you do things. Pay particular attention to the amount of authority you need to obtain to do or buy anything. Ask what's expected of you, and which benchmarks you will be up against fairly soon. Discover the cycle of routine activities: there's nothing worse than being totally unprepared for an end of month report, or being criticized within 2 weeks of starting for not supplying key information to your boss.

Learn as much as you can about policies, procedures, standards – the rules. Conformity may be boring, but it keeps you out of trouble in your first few weeks. It also signals your ability to learn systems quickly – a useful transferable skill. Conformity in new recruits is highly valued because you quickly transform yourself from problem to asset, and you start to look as if you really belong.

When learning, observe and listen, and ask only intelligent questions. Don't expect to be spoon-fed. If you really don't understand a process or task, find someone at your level or a junior level to explain it to you step by step rather than take up a manager's time.

Be careful how far you suggest good ideas at this stage. The basic rule is don't criticize and don't run down the way someone is doing the job now. However, you might be able to make some tentative suggestions of new things that can be done. This is best done on a sharing basis ('Perhaps we could have a chat some time about that ...') rather than telling people how things should be done. Often it's best to sit on your reactions to how things are done, and just focus at this stage on enthusiasm for the job as it stands, throwing in a few additional ideas that add value to the present process rather than challenging it.

If you spot something that appears to be done inefficiently, make a note but don't comment just yet – see **quick wins** below. Commenting immediately marks you out as a smart Alec and a threat, and people will start to be less open.

Working at the people dimension

Don't rely just on your first day grand tour to meet new people. Try to sit next to new colleagues every day at lunch or at coffee. Seize opportunities to visit other departments or branches. When introduced to new colleagues don't just smile and nod, show interest in their jobs and problems, and show you are impressed by what they do. You may be the first person who has really listened to them talk about their jobs for a while. Keep a note of their names and their areas of responsibility. If you're stuck, they will usually respond to a phone call along the lines of 'I'm new here – help me out ...'.

Reading your company's attitude to career development

Something you need to learn early on in the game is how your company thinks about career development. Be aware, of course, that this can be subjective – what is self-development to one person is promotion seeking to another, and 'simply doing a good job' to yet another. There is no such thing as work activity that is not in some way related to career development (or at least, retention) – you're either undertaking activity which encourages your employer to keep you and develop you, or you're committing Career-Limiting Actions. Contrary to popular belief, there's no real middle ground. The favourite strategy of 'getting on with the job' is far from neutral – it often means that you're just treading water.

Plenty of employers talk about career development, but not quite as many really do anything about it. You can begin to find out by looking at your employer's attitude to training: are you able to go on courses? If so, how strictly do they need to be related to your present job content?

Remember that career development is about a lot more than training. For organizations with a well-developed career management programme, what you may be offered is the chance to think about career progression (ideally in a conversation that is not about performance review or short-term objectives). Employers who offer this will tend to give you the opportunity to work with someone who can provide helpful, objective feedback. Very often this will be someone independent of the direct management process; it may even be a mentor who assists you over a longer period.

Remember, however, that an awful lot of employers make large claims about encouraging learning and career development. Some of them have attracted certification or awards (such as the Investors in People scheme in the UK). In all cases, ask around: find out what the organization does, not just what it says.

USING A CAREER AWARENESS STRATEGY IN A NEW JOB

Employment consultant Peter Jackson reminds us that 'the difficulty is that each company has a different culture in terms of attitudes to promotion, with the US style of organization expecting people to put themselves forward for promotion, compared with the British ethos of "waiting till you're selected" otherwise you might appear to be pushy'. It's vital to work out a balance between your style and the style of the organization: how passive or active are you expected to be? In the 21st century there are fewer and fewer companies who are prepared to manage our careers for us. The 'wait and hope' strategy works reasonably well in a paternalistic system, but as each year goes by there are less organizations in the UK that work that way. For good or ill, we are moving towards an economy that requires an active approach to career management, or – as this book suggests, **career awareness** (see **Chapter 3**).

Career awareness is about being aware of yourself *and* deeply aware of organizational reality. In this case, an active approach hunts down information about how far your organization accepts and values behaviours which are clear signals of potential. Each organization has its own style, and its own limits. Using your first few months in the company to find out just this will be time well spent.

Have your finger on the pulse of your company, and work out how things really work there. Don't assume that your new employer will behave like others you have worked for, or like organizations where your friends work. What works in one organization doesn't always work in another. This can be problematic for someone who changes companies and brings to the new culture an attitude to promotion that doesn't travel well.

As you become established it is time to use strategies outlined in **Chapter 2** of this book. Take the advice of Robin Wood, MD of outplacement specialists CMC, who reminds us that you attract the attention of managers by being 'positive, can do, energetic, cheerful, enthusiastic and always prepared to go above and beyond the call of duty'.

Consider doing the OBVIOUS

Use the **OBVIOUS** benchmark in **Table 12.1** to guide your actions in the first few months of your new job.

Table 12.1   Doing the OBVIOUS

Your actions should be:

Observable	others will be talking about what you have achieved
Benchmarked	the effects will be measurable
Visible	to key decision-makers
Individual	the fact that this is *your* personal contribution will be clearly identifiable
On Target	focused on what matters to the organization
Understood	people see the obstacles you had to overcome
Special	something that clearly differentiates you from others, whether external or internal to the organization

Look for quick wins

Once you've got an idea of *what* you need to do to help your company, and how you need to do it, you need to get some quick wins. A quick win is not a motivational gimmick, but a practical reality: what is the most successful activity you can undertake in the shortest time, with the minimum of effort and resources?

New managers going into companies often miss quick wins. They want to put huge strategic changes into effect. These take time, and often meet resistance. Unsuccessful managers often fail because they try to impose a template or an idea on an organization without investigating how it already works – or doesn't. Others know better.

The best way is to walk around and talk to people about the work they do. Ask them for things that can be fixed quickly. Ask around – what gets in the way of productivity? What can be resolved obviously and cheaply? Often existing staff know exactly what's going wrong. They will identify 'just this one small thing' that gets in the way; and it's usually about doing something very simply and immediately improving either efficiency or customer satisfaction. Talk to people on the shopfloor, particularly those who are customer facing, and ask 'What could we do better?' and 'What are we missing?' The answers are often enlightening. Staff say things like 'I've told the management, but …'.

Pick out one or two of these, check out if the problem and solution are real, and move ahead. But don't forget to give praise and credit to the person who gave you the idea. Decide, or seek permission, to implement two or three changes which are low on cost and high on imagination. Remember, quick wins need to be chosen carefully, because they must be prompt and they must be successful. And make sure you follow-up – don't be a one-hit wonder.

Look for leverage

No matter how fit or energetic you are, you can only commit a finite amount of energy to work. In fact, working longer and longer hours will only produce limited benefits, and ultimately will degrade your performance and your health. If you really want to work smarter, not harder, focus on the projects which make the biggest difference and have the biggest impact.

The next step, once you start to become established, is described by occupational psychologist Derek Wilkie of Stuart Robertson Associates: 'Identify an area of work that is currently or will be a strategic focus for the organization and demonstrate competence, or make progress in working towards the strategic objective'. There is an element of luck here in 'catching the wave' – gaining the right competencies at the right moment. However, if you demonstrate career awareness you're far more likely to see the right moment. As **Chapter 5** indicates, it's important to have a strategic focus and to spot Key Result Areas. 'Catching the wave' is often about tuning in to the major concerns, if not obsessions, of key decision-makers. Derek Wilkie adds: 'Identify who is influential in the organization and find ways of working with them (often quite easy as these people often start initiatives and seek people who are keen to help them achieve them, regardless of organizational hierarchy). Achieve a major new project/initiative/goal. Seek the advice of a internal mentor (formal or informal).'

New start with a new boss

Changes of senior staff are frequent. If you get a new boss, see it as an opportunity to try a new approach. Many people find, in fact, that having a new boss is a really great opportunity to be seen differently. It may also be an opportunity to shine in a new way. Offer solutions, not problems, and you will make an impression fast.

Since a new boss is likely to be very keen to want an overview of the job, this is your chance to talk about the way you contribute to the big picture. Doing that often means that you can negotiate to do more of the things you do well and enthusiastically, and ask to delegate some tasks you find less interesting.

'MUST DO' LIST

☑ Begin to shape your job even from the job offer stage.

☑ Work at the first steps you take in your next job.

☑ Who are the information brokers in your organization? How can you get them on your side?

☑ What career development opportunities does your employer offer?

☑ Who will provide you with career development support? Can you find a mentor – either formally or informally?

☑ What quick wins can you achieve in your present position?

Ten Steps Towards Taking Control of Your Career

This chapter helps you to:

▌ Focus on your next steps

▌ Put together a career development plan for the next 6 months

▌ Take on board top tips from experienced managers and coaches

Tomorrow is often the busiest day of the week

Spanish proverb

STEPPING FORWARD: YOUR 10-STEP PROGRAMME

The following steps build on the key areas of this book and draw on the above summary of what is most likely to be successful as your next move. The steps are punctuated with further useful insights from our career survey.

Step 1: Invest in yourself

Put time aside to review, plan and investigate possibilities for your future. Think of yourself as a solo company. If a company is going downhill it needs to look carefully at its products and services. You, too, can do something similar if you feel you're not making progress. Act as if you were the biggest shareholder in 'Me Plc' – that way you will see the benefits of a regular progress check. Spend at least a day a quarter focusing on your job – cataloguing your successes, looking at areas where you can add to your learning. It also helps you to stock your lifeboat in case you need to jump ship.

☑ Recognize that a sound and steady career progression will be ultimately more satisfying that taking on too much responsibility and failing to deliver'. Lynda Pickess, Sales Director, Manpower UK

Step 2: Know the organization

As we've discussed there's no point focusing on your own strengths unless you know what the organization needs. Think about your organization's headaches, worries, opportunities and goals. Use the checklist in **Chapter 5** to spot the gaps you have in your organizational knowledge. Find out as much as you can using your own resources – imagine all your life savings were about to be invested in this organization, and look at it accordingly. Find out who the key information brokers are within the organization. Most people operate largely in the dark, but there will be key people who know virtually everything and everyone.

☑ 'Know the business, where the important pieces of work that have the greatest impact are taking place and move towards developing knowledge in those areas.' HR professional Breda O'Toole

☑ 'Talk to people in different jobs to ensure you know what they entail. Find out what these jobs need and if you could make an impression by doing them. **Never** choose a job because it sounds important – you must be able to do well in it.' Rob Head, formerly Corporate Development Manager, Octel Corp

Step 3: Watch the politics

This is a key survival activity. Organizational survivors are often not those with the best skills, but those who are most keenly tuned to office politics. The ones who become discarded are all too often the people who can't read the writing on the wall. Understand what your boss really wants in life, and help to provide it. Be very careful around new bosses, re-establish your presence just as if you were starting a new job.

☑ 'Look at your role and the organization as a whole: what can be improved on, implemented and have a direct result to the success of the company? What will you be remembered for?' Justine Wilkinson, IT Recruitment Consultant

☑ 'Do the current job so well that people entrust you with more than the job content.' John Courtis, Director of search and selection firm Courtis & Partners Ltd.

Step 4: Be an ideas machine

Don't be blinkered by your own industry sector. Beg, steal or borrow great ideas from other environments. Keep up to date: read widely, hunt down useful contacts, go to exhibitions and conferences. Become hungry for new information about your sector and about your client base, and keep people informed that you are doing so. Collate and summarize key information – be seen as an information broker. Setting up an e-group (Yahoo and Hotmail offer simple solutions) around a particular subject is easy, free, and gets results – it enables a group of people with a common interest to share ideas and post questions. It's no substitute for face-to-face networking, but it can help you grow your range of contacts.

☑ 'Work out what problem your boss has (the deep down one) and provide a solution for that, without becoming a threat to him.' Philip Spencer, Consumer marketing expert

Step 5: Adopt a strategy for rejection

We know that even the best sales performers get a 'no' from about four out of five prospects. The trick is to learn how to cope with rejection and focus on the winning outcomes. When we investigate possibilities for promotion or ask for new responsibilities, we may come up against objections or outright refusal. We need to learn from rejections rather than using them as an excuse to stick with the *status quo*.

☑ 'Decide on a plan of action and stick to it. Ensure your boss knows what your immediate ambitions are.' Stephen Hunter, Commercial and NHS Trust Board Chairman

Step 6: Communicate a clear message

Learn the art of self-marketing – making sure that you communicate three key messages: (1) what you do well, (2) how you make a difference, and (3) the kinds of challenges and projects you'd like to take on so your job will develop.

☑ 'Communicate well. It has to be known that you are delivering without stuffing your performance down people throats.' Alan Small, Outplacement Consultant

Step 7: Fall forwards

Don't be afraid of making mistakes; it's all part of the process. The important thing is to fall forwards, not backwards – in other words, learn from your false starts. Keep looking for new angles, new possibilities for your next 'offer'. You will end up very focused, very clear about what you want to do next. Employers really buy into this level of confidence.

☑ 'Winning the argument is not always the best solution to some situations. Presenting 'options' and 'potential solutions' demonstrates a willingness to take responsibility to help solve problems and think creatively towards supporting other members of the team.' Deirdre Hughes, Director, Centre for Guidance Studies, University of Derby

Step 8: Recruit your dream team

Every top sports performer needs a dream team: a coach, a personal trainer, experienced athletes, motivators, managers.

Who can help you? At the very least, recruit some positive-thinking friends to support you through your exploration, your discoveries, and to help you cope with the ups and downs of job search. It's the only way of getting past the constraints we identified in **Chapter 3** – the barriers that get in the way, the internal voices that tell you that you won't succeed. The biggest barriers to career change are ones you create yourself. Remember also that those close to you at home also need to be on board, to understand what you're doing and to keep you confident.

☑ 'Don't win in business and lose in life – your family and friends deserve more than what left after you've give your best to your work and they'll still be there when the job's gone.' Joëlle Warren, Director of Executive Recruitment Consultancy Warren Partners

Step 9: Keep making connections

Successful sales people and recruiters know step 9 well. Set time aside to maintain relationships. Keep careful records of your contacts, and keep in touch at least once every 6 months. Cultivate the people who are already at the centre of great networks – the people who know everybody and know what's happening before it happens. The early tip-off often makes the difference between being a leader and being a follower.

☑ 'Deliver what is important to your boss. Work hard to do what you do now very well and be recognized for it. Be in the right place at the right time.' Outplacement Consultant Bill Hollyhead

☑ 'It's very hard, but I recommend authenticity as the best career strategy. Not because it makes you a better person – although it does – but because it makes you much better at whatever you're good at, and gives you a genuine point of difference. Think for yourself.' Maureen Rice-Knight

Step 10: Step out

Once you've got the key preparation stages sorted out, start thinking about activity. Make sure your plan for the perfect promotion isn't just a textbook event. What training experiences can you arrange? Who do you need to consult or influence? How are you going to begin to increase your exposure? *What are you going to do now that you have finished this book?*

☑ 'Develop a strategy to achieve it; develop a strategy if you don't. Either way, follow through.' Melissa Rosati, Publishing Executive

The overall message? In the game of survivor, take responsibility for your future. If you want an average career with average career satisfaction, continue the passive route. If you want to create real choices, take control; an employer is responsible for getting the best out of you, but no one else will look after your career but you.

Useful Websites

Unless stated otherwise, these websites provide free and often downloadable information about career development issues.

LINKS TO JOHN LEES WEBSITES

www.jobyoulove.co.uk
www.johnleescareers.com
For full details of John Lees' work and a wide range of career development tips

CAREER DEVELOPMENT, EXPLORATION AND MANAGEMENT

www.sr-associates.com
For an online opportunity to take Quintax, the personality measure outlined in **Chapter 3**

http://content.monster.co.uk/career_development
Monster Career Centre with advice and information on Career Development, Salaries & Benefits, Workplace Issues and Changing Careers

http://education.independent.co.uk/careers_advice
The Independents Careers Advice mainly aimed at graduates. The site also contains links and information on MBAs

http://jobs.guardian.co.uk/careerscentre
The Guardian's Career Centre. Articles on all aspects of
career management

www.acinet.org
America's Career InfoNet is a resource for making informed
career decisions

www.alljobsuk.com
Comprehensive Internet signpost in searching for your next
career move

www.askmen.co.uk/money/index.html
Lifestyle portal for Men. Wide range of articles (with a
US bias) on career management and issues surrounding
the workplace

www.bbc.co.uk/business/work/index.shtml
Work and careers information

www.careersfair.com/
Job sites, careers advice, recruitment agencies, careers
services, courses and professional bodies - Thousands of
UK, European and worldwide links

www.careerjournal.com/
Executive Career Site produced by the *Wall Street Journal*

www.careers.lon.ac.uk/
Advice, guidance, information, events, links and other
services for graduate job-seekers

www.careerplanner.com/
US Site provides online career tests, free career planning
information, advice and ideas plus other chargeable services

www.careers-portal.co.uk
Online Careers service covering advice and information
about higher education and alternatives also choosing and
managing your career

www.careeroink.com
A career guidance website with a database that uses
information from a variety of sources from the
US Department of Labor

http://www.connexions-direct.com/jobs4u/home.cfm
Information on different types of careers

www.handbag.com/careers/careerprogression
Advice for working women covering change your career,
improving your salary, enjoy your job, coping with your boss

http://www.dol.gov
US Department of Labor – Information and links to a range
of career resources

www.ideasfactory.com/index.htm
Careers insights and advice from real-life professionals and
practical information for careers in the creative field

www.ivillage.co.uk/workcareer
Career advice for women

www.jobsandmoms.com/
Career resources tailored to working mothers in search of
more family friendly work options and new career directions

http://www.mindtools.com/pages/main/newMN_TMC.htm
Career Guidance and downloaded resources on career and
life skills such as Time Management, Problem Solving and
Decision making along side many others

www.timesonline.co.uk/career
The Times' career section contains practical career advice

www.totaljobs.com/editorial/getadvice/index.shtm
Job board which also contains career management advice
and a salary checker

www.workthing.com/
Jobs & advice split into industry specialisms with guidance
on career development

TRAINING

www.direct.gov.uk/Topics/Learning/AdultLearners/fs/en
Directgov offers advice for adults returning to learning with
ideas about, what, where and how to study plus advice
about financial help available

www.learndirect.co.uk
Advice on courses available online and through UK
Universities and Colleges

www.lifelonglearning.co.uk/
Information on lifelong learning and the UK governments
initiatives

www.prospects.ac.uk
Graduate careers website. Information on types of jobs and
industries along with careers advice and guidance. Also
includes information on post-graduate courses

WORK/LIFE BALANCE

www.dti.gov.uk/work-lifebalance/
UK Government website offering advice and guidance on
work life balance

www.dti.gov.uk/er/workingparents.htm
UK Government website offering guidance to working
parents

CAREER BREAKS

http://www.handbag.com/careers/careerbreak/studyleave
General advice on taking a career break or leaving work to
study

http://www.yearoutgroup.org
Information and ideas for those interested in taking a year
out from their studies

http://www.bbc.co.uk/holiday/tv_and_radio/
grown_up_gappers
Information for 'grown up gappers'

WORKPLACE ISSUES

www.e-reputation.co.uk/
Site under development
A collection of free downloads on Improving your
communication skills, persuading others and survival tips
in the workplace

www.emplaw.co.uk
Includes summaries of key points of employment law

www.hayspersonnel.com/content/candidate/advice/
your_raise.jsp
Article on negotiating a pay rise; further articles and links
to careers advice and salary surveys

www.hse.gov.uk/stress
Health & Safety Executive website on workplace stress

www.officepolitics.co.uk
Humorous site based on *The Guardian*'s weekend column
authored by Guy Browning about the absurdities of
working life

www.tiger.gov.uk
Guide to UK employment law

www.workstress.net
Website covering work-related stress, its causes and how to
eliminate it

NETWORKING

www.afpoe.com
A directory, which lists the skills, knowledge and know-
how of its worldwide membership

http://beyondbricks.ecademy.com/index.php
Business exchange that connects people to knowledge &
contacts globally

www.zoominfo.com
Source of people information

http://www.magicof.co.uk
Site offering guidance on Networking

www.homealoners.co.uk
Social and professional networking for those who work at
home

EXPLORING ALTERATIVE OPTIONS TO EMPLOYMENT

www.businesslink.org
Advice on setting up and running a business, including
funding and grants

www.bvca.co.uk
British Venture Capital Association

www.chamberonline.co.uk
British Chamber of Commerce

www.companieshouse.gov.uk/info
Guidance on Setting up a business and how to register a
Business Name

www.bcuk.co.uk
Business Clubs UK

www.cbi.org.uk
CBI

www.dwp.gov.uk
Department for Work and Pensions

www.dti.gov.uk
Department of Trade & Industry

www.fsb.org.uk
Federation of Small Businesses (FSB)

www.flexibility.co.uk
Resources and information for those exploring new ways of working such as portfolio work and home working

www.homeworking.com/
Information about working from home

www.inlandrevenue.gov.uk
Inland Revenue New Business Starter Pack

members.aol.com
Institute of Inventors

www.invent.org.uk
Institute of Patentees and Inventors

www.icaew.co.uk
ICAEW – help with choosing an accountant

www.icof.co.uk
A company providing loan finance for co-operatives, employee-owned businesses and community enterprises

www.lawsoc.org.uk
Law Society – help with choosing a solicitor

www.bestmatch.co.uk
National Business Angels Network

www.nfea.com
Enterprise agencies are local not-for-profit organizations that help new and small businesses

www.startups.co.uk
Information and advice for people wanting to start their own business

www.ukbi.co.uk
Business incubators provide start-up help for new businesses in return for a stake in the company

VOLUNTARY WORK

www.charitiesdirect.com
A Charities Database, providing regularly updated
information on over 10,000 UK charities

www.cns.gov
Corporation for National and Community Service engages
Americans of all ages and backgrounds to volunteer

www.csv.org.uk
UK largest volunteering and training organization

www.idealist.org
Over 44,000 non-profit and community organizations in
165 countries, which you can search. Directory of Volunteer
opportunities around the world, and a list of organizations

www.timebank.org.uk
Information on voluntary opportunities in the UK

www.voluntarywork.org
International directory of voluntary work organizations

Index